INSIDE
THE PLAZA

INSIDE
THE PLAZA

AN INTIMATE PORTRAIT OF THE ULTIMATE HOTEL

WARD MOREHOUSE III

APPLAUSE
NEW YORK • LONDON

AN APPLAUSE ORIGINAL

INSIDE THE PLAZA
AN INTIMATE PORTRAIT OF THE ULTIMATE HOTEL
BY WARD MOREHOUSE III

Copyright © 2001 by Ward Morehouse III

COVER INSET PHOTOS: Marilyn Monroe and Laurence Olivier;
Elizabeth Taylor and Richard Burton: both, PHOTOFEST

Library of Congress Cataloguing-in-Publication Data
Library of Congress Card Number: 2001092421

British Library Cataloguing-in-Publication Data
A catalogue record for this book is available from the
British Library

ISBN: 1-55783-468-7
Printed in Canada

APPLAUSE BOOKS
151 West 46th Street
New York, NY 10036
Phone: 212-575-9265
Fax: 646-562-5852
email: info@applausepub.com

COMBINED BOOK SERVICES LTD.
Units I/K, Paddock Wood Distribution Centre
Paddock Wood, Tonbridge, Kent TN 12 6UU
Phone: (44) 01892 837171
Fax: (44) 01892 837272
United Kingdom

SALES & DISTRIBUTION:
HAL LEONARD CORP.
7777 West Bluemound Road
P. O. Box 13819
Milwaukee, WI 53213
Phone: 1-414-774-3630
Fax: 1-414-774-3259
email: halinfo@halleonard.com
internet: www.halleonard.com

FOR LIZ,

AND FOR WILL,
who will know The Plaza
and other hotels of the next half century —
I hope they will be as exciting for him as
they have been for me

CONTENTS

ACKNOWLEDGMENTS

The author wishes to thank current and past managers of The Plaza, notably Gary Schweikert, the hotel's current vice-president and general manager, Tom Civitano, the hotel's vice-president of sales and marketing, Richard Wilhelm, who managed The Plaza under Donald and Ivana Trump and Philip Hughes, who was brought in by Westin International and managed The Plaza from 1976 to 1984, for their support and extraordinary amount of time they spent being interviewed for this book. Also, I am indebted to current owners of The Plaza, Chairman Kwek Leng Beng and Prince Alwaleed Bin Talal, for their interviews and assistance; to Donald Trump, a past owner; William Fatt, chairman of Fairmont Hotels and Resorts; and to Plaza Asset Manager Paul Underhill. Also, special thanks for research to The New York Historical Society, The Museum of the City of New York, The Beinecke Rare Book Library, Yale University, the special collections of the Princeton University Libraries, The Library at the Cornell University School of Hotel Administration, The Rhode Island Historical Society, Nancy Battet, "heritage director" of Fairmont Hotels and Resorts, the archives of *The New York Times*, The New York *Post* and my father, Ward Morehouse's biography of George M. Cohan, *Prince of the American Theater*.

I also wish to thank the countless people who provided me with their personal memories of living in and working at The Plaza, including my mother Joan Marlowe Rahe, stepmother, Rebecca Morehouse, and Fred Cristina, maitre d' of the Oak Room, Lawrence Harvey, Jeffrey Jacobs, Joseph Szorentini, Paul Nicaj, Joseph Trombetti, Clint Wade, Regina Henry, Lee Solters, Harvey Sabinson, George Lang, Martin Riskin, Curtis Gathje, Barry Cregan, Geraldine Sheppard and the late Frank

Wangeman and the late Alphonse Salomone.

Special thanks also to Neil Simon, Hilary Knight, Rosemary Clooney, Bob Hope, Gloria Vanderbilt, Sylvia Miles, Julie Wilson, Andrea Marcovicci, Leslie Gore, Monique Van Voren, Peter Duchin, Donald Smith, Kenn Viselman, Brooke Astor, Martin Richards, Margaret Whiting, Don Dellair, Elizabeth Morehouse, Stewart Lane, Bonnie Comley, Howard Sandum, Roderic W. Rahe, Clifford Wattley, Glenn Young, Kay Radtke, Greg Collins, Glynn Lewis, Betty Blake, Sy Preston, Dick McSherry, Leonard Finger, Patricia Sheppard Patterson, William Morehouse, Charles Barrett, Blanche Sockwell, Christina Krupka, Melissa Dribben, Paul Tharp, Ken Chandler, John Hueffner, Ellis Nassour, Bill Hoffman, Matt Diebel, Gregory Lamb, Gail Parenteau, the late Arthur Cantor, William H. Carr and many others.

PROLOGUE

An emerald-topped, eighteen-story-tall wedding cake set down upon the shore of a sea of green trees, The Plaza Hotel is one of the Crown Jewels of New York City. Its expressway-wide corridors, its ballroom-high ceilings, its unimpeded panoramic views of Central Park and Fifth Avenue, make its guests feel like royalty — even those who aren't.

As a young boy living at the hotel, I thought The Plaza went on forever, a never-ending pastiche of elegant rooms and magnificently lit corridors strung together like the most finely wrought diamond necklace. As I walked, or more likely ran, down those long, long hallways to my father's suite, I fantasized some wonderful romantic tale ongoing behind each stately door: a Russian countess here, a star ballerina there; maybe an actor rehearsing his lines or a writer hunched over his typewriter concocting the next *Great Gatsby*. Everyone in this castle was exotic to me. Food just appeared in silver dishes and mints miraculously surfaced upon fluffy pillows. The Plaza Hotel was big in every way, but especially big with blessings.

What follows is a highly personalized "people" biography of this grandest of grand hotels. It is also a story of hundreds of dreams all bound together, sometimes by the thinnest of threads, and other times, by history and traditions centuries in the making.

⌘

The Plaza has, give or take a suite or two, 805 keys for suites and single rooms. Former manager Wilhelm explains this as, "there are 1,000 cubicles, 1,000 rooms, but there are quite a few one- and two- and three-bedroom suites. And so there are really 815 'keys,' which as you know is really the front door to any particular group of units . . . 805 keys but to 1,000 rooms." One could accurately state, of course, that The Plaza has never been completed architecturally, and never will be. The exact number of rooms at The Plaza has shifted dramatically every year of its existence. But however you tabulate them, they range from baronial suites so large they contain their own corridors, to intimate rooms shyly facing the elegant white-brick interior courtyard, in the manner of Paris's fabled Plaza Athenee.

The hotel's several famous restaurants echo with the voices of the famous and the fabulous. The new One C.P.S., formerly The Edwardian Room, overlooking the Fifth Avenue and Central Park South corner of the hotel, has the added distinction of being one of the most romantic dining rooms in the country. The Oak Room, with its similarly vaulted ceiling and old British men's club aura, was a favorite of George M. Cohan, Cary Grant, Gary Cooper, Humphrey Bogart, Lauren Bacall, Joe DiMaggio, Marilyn Monroe, James Cagney, and more recently, Stevie Wonder, Liza Minnelli, and Dudley Moore. And the Palm Court may just be the world's most beautiful dining space. Paul Goldberger, former architecture critic of *The New York Times*, has said, "The Plaza is surely the most beloved public building in New York."

Every great hotel has its legends, but The Plaza has had many of its preserved, or created, on stage and on screen. A singularly gorgeous structure situated on the most exquisite point of real estate in New York, it has proven an irresistible magnet to dramatists and directors over the years. Dozens of movies and plays have "taken place" within or around this landmark.

New York's "other" grand hotel, The Waldorf-Astoria, has been called "America's Gilded Dream." But The Plaza is more like a dream itself than stone and steel, a magical space as well as place, a trip to the imagination. Perhaps that's why the dream-factory folk, like Warren Beatty, Madonna, Eddie Murphy, Elizabeth Taylor and the late Richard Burton, or, going back a bit, earlier New York icons like Vanderbilt, Hardenbergh, Sterry and Fitzgerald, have felt so at home there.

On the other hand, many of the famous have come here to get *away* from the noise and fuss of being well-known, namely, film star Greta Garbo, architect Frank Lloyd Wright and playwright Ferenc Molnar.

The Plaza is a fantasy realm where you can play out whatever role you wish to, whether that be commoner as royalty, or royalty as just plain folks.

But it is also America's great democratic palace, where hard work or just plain hard cash will get you the same room, the same special service as that received by the rich and famous. In fact, while a one-bedroom so-called "Plaza Suite" on the corner of Fifth Avenue and Central Park South may be $1800 a night, it's still possible to get much smaller accommodations at The Plaza for rates comparable to other much less famous hotels. For instance, a small room with a bathroom almost as big as the bedroom, and facing the hotel's inside court instead of Fifth Avenue or Central Park, runs less than a few hundred dollars. (When the hotel opened you could get a single room without bath for $2.50. A bath was $1.50 extra.)

Structurally, The Plaza's famously thick walls play a large part in facilitating these assorted private fantasies. The hotel is actually three-sided with a cavernous "well" in the middle — much like the balconies of a theatre facing a stage. Except, in this case, all the drama is going on in the seats not on the boards.

It's also a place that never seems to age, adding to the dreamlike atmosphere. It is always current, never out of fashion, never behind the times, and somehow, in true fairy-tale style, always outside of time. It is a place where F. Scott Fitzgerald is forever not growing up, memorably thrashing around in the Pulitzer Fountain. It is a place where Lillian Russell is forever leaving her diamond studded bicycle out in front of the 59th Street entrance with the doorman, a place where, in the third millennium, horse-drawn hansom cabs still pull up at the front door to whisk you away with Belle Epoque panache.

Have a stroll down Fifth Avenue on a cool summer night and you may see some of the things that have changed over the years (unprotected, alas, by The Plaza's magic spell). Office buildings have replaced many of the limestone mansions, particularly the Vanderbilt mansion. If you were fortunate enough, many years ago, you would have seen the vast Vanderbilt mansion on the site where Bergdorf-Goodman now stands. The mansion was once the crowning glory of old-world wealth.

And yet, on that same summer stroll, you may see many things that have remained the same. At Fifth Avenue and 55th Street, for example, you might feel as if you could almost walk back to the turn of the century. To the east and to the west, you are flanked by the famous St. Regis Hotel and The Peninsula (formerly called The Gotham). These hotels were among the first of New York's "skyscraper" hotels, of which The Plaza became the ultimate the model.

The Plaza is also about "arriving," one way or another. Whether you are literary geniuses like F. Scott Fitzgerald and Dorothy Parker, or Lee Iococca who brought back The Chrysler Corporation from the dead, or a topnotch tie-salesman from Omaha, The Plaza is a place to celebrate and be celebrated.

One thing The Plaza is not about, however, is "departing." It knows that it departs from its near century-long tradition at great risk; and it never thinks of its clients as leaving the hotel, at least not permanently — the staff's every activity is devoted toward making guests not only feel at home but making them long to return.

※

My own story of "arriving" at The Plaza begins properly with my extensive personal experience of living there. As a young boy, then young man, then young newspaper reporter and later as a theater columnist and drama critic, The Plaza was just home. Truly home. It wasn't the fantasy world, it wasn't the brilliantly shining yet unapproachable star it was to others, Donald Trump among them. It was just home. Nor did I perceive myself as some whimsical character out of Kay Thompson's famous Eloise stories. I was a kid. I thought everybody lived in eighteen-story public palaces with great room service.

My mother and father lived at the hotel before I was born, then my father resided there for eleven years with my stepmother, Rebecca Franklin Morehouse. I was forever visiting them.

Maybe even more than The Waldorf-Astoria, where my parents also lived, my life has been wrapped up in The Plaza Hotel. Part of this, of course, was wishful thinking. Part of it is the genuine memory of the actual events that occurred there. I can remember my mother, for instance, telling me of a now long gone and forgotten restaurant, called the Rooftop Restaurant, that she used to observe from the window of her suite on the 58th Street side of the hotel. Then, as I began this book, I started to become, in my imagination, some of the characters who have graced the marble hallways of this amazing building.

My first memories of the hotel were, as I said, of visiting my father, a noted drama critic and columnist in his own right, along with my nurse maid/companion, Anna. (Who used to say she was "from Hunger" whenever anyone asked after her place of origin.) To me, The Plaza was just another part of my Central Park playground, where there were miles of incredible wonders to explore and experience. Behind every hill was romance. Not the kind I was to learn about later, but that feeling forever associated with childhood, very much like a fairy tale. It was the feeling of something new and different happening and there was no past or future, but only the present, only the now.

As a Broadway columnist and roving correspondent, my father stayed in so many hotels in his lifetime that he once suggested the words, "Room Service, Please!" be inscribed on his tombstone. He actually stayed, including The Plaza, at some thirty hotels in New York alone. "I'm not a rich man," he used to say. "But I live like a millionaire."

Like the real millionaires, he was attracted by The Plaza's grandeur and elegance and he loved being in beautiful surroundings. He also never forgot his long interview sessions with George M. Cohan at the great man's corner table in the Oak Room, where the great entertainer would regale friends with stories of his life on the road and on Broadway in various shows. One night in the Thirties Cohan broke into a refrain of his own song "I'm a Yankee Doodle Dandy!" He received a standing ovation even though by then he'd largely turned his talents to acting in comedies and not musicals and his voice was not what it had been. (When a Metropolitan Opera singer was asked to sing a few high notes some twenty years later, maitre d' Victor pleaded, "No high notes, please! Remember the china!")

My stepmother once said that the interior suite she and my father had may have been too much "like a cave" and actually contributed to my father's drinking. It overlooked the hotel's interior court instead of a view of Central Park, Fifth Avenue or 58th Street. When I was small it looked very grandiose indeed. When I took a look at it in March, 2000 — the maid let me have a peek at both rooms — it looked rather small. I could, however, see clearly that the kitchen where we lit gunpowder had been turned into a bathroom although it seemed that the same white tile was there which had been in the kitchen.

"Chester Dale lived on my floor and there was a duchess across the hall," recalls my stepmother, a former *Time* and Atlanta *Journal* staff writer. Dale was a utilities financier who, at the time he lived in his sixth floor Plaza suite, had what was considered the finest private collection of French modern art in the world, including Claude Monet's *The Old Musician*. "The Plaza liked to have people live there who gave it a certain sheen," my stepmother continued. "People are so impressed that I lived at The Plaza. 'You lived at The Plaza for 11 years? I don't believe!' They're amazed."

My father had loved The Plaza from the time he first set foot in Manhattan in 1919 and began working for the old New York *Tribune*. He visited there often, especially with his pal George M. (After Cohan died in 1942 my father wrote the best biography of him ever done.) My father stayed there occasionally with this or that chorus girl he wanted to impress but didn't live there until he and my mother, actress Joan Marlowe, lived in a large suite on the 58th Street side of the hotel for several years. They paid less than $100 a month. My mother, the "natural one," was a former Broadway actress and theatrical publisher and editor.

From 1950 to 1961 he lived there with my stepmother at a rate of $300 a month for their one-bedroom suite, a rate that was quite a bargain at a time when the "rack rate" or normal rate for the suite was more than $1000 a month. Part of the reason he got a discount is that he'd mention the hotel frequently in his "Broadway After Dark" column in the New York *Sun*. They lived at The Plaza for eleven years. My memories of Rebecca of this time period are somewhat sketchy, although we became very close after my father died. I do recall that when I'd visit my father in the hotel, she'd be propped up with a lot of pillows in bed. Looking back. I suppose she reminded me of Jean Harlow — pampered but regal.

Long before he lived at The Plaza, my father occupied a cavernous suite at the Art Deco Essex House (completed in 1931 on Central Park South.) He paid the then king's ransom of $300 a month for a huge two-bedroom suite overlooking Central Park.

Having made a small fortune writing early "talkies," including *Up in Central Park*, and consulting on the screenplay of his play *Gentlemen of the Press*, my father could afford to live lavishly there with his second wife, Broadway producer Jean Dalrymple, in a suite on the 38th floor facing Central Park that would have done an MGM sound stage proud.

A bevy of stage and screen beauties streamed into the hotel suite every night and on any given night the author of the celebrated "Broadway After Dark" column was trading fashionable insults of the day with Dorothy Parker, Alexander Woollcott or Miriam Hopkins (another of my father's girlfriends). When his wife complained that he'd sent a big Broadway star a hundred roses, he bought the entire stock of the Essex House florist and had it sent up to their suite.

On Saturdays, when I'd visit father, at whatever hotel he was staying, we'd take in maybe three, or four, or five Broadway plays a day. Sometimes we'd just watch fifteen or twenty minutes of one, then leave for the next. Father was a tougher critic than I. Of course, there were a lot more shows on Broadway in those days. Sometimes the show was sold out, for everyone but father that is. There was always a seat for him, but not necessarily for me — to make up for it the theatre manager would bring me a special chair to plop down in the middle of the aisle next to father's anchored aisle seat. Talk about a seat on the aisle. I had one in the aisle. It was exactly this sense of privilege I'd felt at The Plaza. Only, as yet, I was still too young to realize, much less appreciate, it.

My father, like Fitzgerald, like Dorothy Parker, was a child not only at heart but also down to his soul. He reveled in being alive, and in all the wondrous possibilities of hotel living with everything, including room service, at your fingertips. At The Plaza my father even kept a bear in the kitchen of his suite until the maids complained and the pet was packed off to a Georgia farm. My father had already given me a lion cub from South Africa and promised me a baby wolf.

Besides regular visits to The Plaza as a child, I spent several weeks living at the hotel while I collected research material and wrote part of this book. On one such visit I occupied a corner suite on the corner of 59th Street and Bergdorf-Goodman, although I must say I'm forever envisioning the long lost Vanderbilt mansion where Bergdorf's stands today.

My suite's living room alone, with its marble fireplace (bricked up years ago to meet modern fire code and insurance requirements), has as many square feet as a small but comfortable two-bedroom apartment in the average modern rental apartment building. The bathroom, with its vaulted barrel-shaped ceiling, itself is the size of a bedroom in such an apartment. The bedroom, with canopy bed, is also large but not cavernous, as the living room seems to be.

At the moment, snow covers Fifth Avenue and Pulitzer Fountain. Karl Bitter's statue of Pomona, the Roman goddess of abundance, wears a shawl of white. (The fountain, in memory of but also paid for by newspaper czar Joseph Pulitzer, was installed in 1916.) Scott Fitzgerald wouldn't frolic in her wavelets in this kind of weather. But even through the thick glass of the suite's huge windows you can hear, around the corner at 59th Street and Fifth Avenue, the clippity-clop of the horses pulling their flamboyantly festooned carriages.

A few days later I moved to a suite on the Central Park side of the hotel and there was a very different feel. Facing Fifth Avenue, I had the sense of somehow being protected by familiar city landmarks. In other words, despite its size, there was an unmistakable "cozy" air.

Facing the park, you discover sixty blocks of forests and glens and lakes spread out before you through the billiard-table-sized windows. It gave me the feeling of being a bird tucked into a niche high in a cliff. In one sense it was not like being in the city at all. It could have been one of those vast "railroad hotels" in Canada built at the turn-of-the-century and serviced by luxury trains — or on a lake in Switzerland.

In November of 2000, I came back to the hotel to stay for several days in the "Plaza Suite," the corner suite facing both Fifth Avenue and Central Park. From the living room, looking diagonally across Central Park, I could spy The Dakota apartment house at 72nd Street and Central Park West — also designed by Henry Hardenbergh — where Rosemary had her baby and John Lennon met his untimely, unseemly end. I had a great feeling of continuity about The Plaza, New York and my life.

The Plaza, meanwhile, had undergone a metamorphosis from the early 1990s, when it was struggling just to survive. It now enjoyed the luxury and freedom of a determined ownership and management team, a spirit reflected in every detail from the extremely courteous and able staff to the renovation of the suites, restaurants and all public rooms. It had returned to its original, aristocratic glory.

"From the very beginning The Plaza was an institution, and the legend of its being, richly upholstered in the manners and possessions of the celebrated and wealthy of the world, has continued in unabated magnificence from that time right down to the immediate here and now," the late, illustrious New York writer and genial raconteur Lucius Beebe wrote on the occasion of The Plaza's 50th anniversary in 1957. "It is a continuity with the past, more than anything else, which lays hold upon the imagination at the mention of The Plaza . . . the world has grown gray . . . But the lights of The Plaza, somehow and miraculously, have been undimmed. They gleam in welcome across the asphaltine stretches of the wealthiest avenue of the world."

The older I get, the more I appreciate my privileged connection to this grandest of hostelries. But far more fascinating stories than mine have taken place here over the past nearly one hundred years. Some even boggle the imagination — only fitting in a fairy-tale setting. So sit back while I attempt to emulate the fabled Plaza service and provide you with a four-star room-service guide to the world's most storied hotel.

Laying the Foundation —
High Society, High Finance,
High Risk

The story of The Plaza must begin with the Vanderbilts. No, it wasn't the sort of direct financial link William Waldorf Astor and his cousin John Jacob Astor IV (who built the Astoria addition to the old Waldorf) had with the Waldorf-Astoria, but the Vanderbilts virtually owned Fifth Avenue from 51st Street to 58th Street at the time the original Plaza (the first of two) was put up in 1890 on the site of a gentlemen's ice-skating pond — one of the few places the railroad kings didn't own.

The Vanderbilts' "six blocks of splendor," as the cluster of homesteads was called, began with Cornelius Vanderbilt. "Commodore" Vanderbilt, the family patriarch, started his business with a saill boat called a periauger, eventually seizing control of boat traffic between Manhattan and Staten Island. (More than a century later the funeral for yachtsman and horse breeder Alfred Vanderbilt, the Commodore's great-grandson, was held on Staten Island from whence the empire originally set sail.) The Commodore then moved his ambitions onto dry land, assembling small rail lines into a huge conglomerate.

His son, William H. Vanderbilt, doubled his father's fortune to more than $200 million, a Bill Gatesian-size pile in those days. Then, about the time this Bill's sons started to take an interest in dad's business affairs, it was time to start carving up the most desirable chunks of Manhattan real estate to provide the clan with suitable homes and gardens.

Willie K's brother Cornelius N. would outdo them all with his palatial red brick and white stone mansion at 1 West 57th Street, which he extended north to 58th Street a decade later in 1892. Razed in 1927 to make way for Bergdorf-Goodman's store, the mansion and southeast corner of The Plaza was romantically depicted in Everett Shinn's nostalgic mural which still adorns the hotel's Oak Bar. (Shinn, a former newspaper sketch artist, was a member of the so-called Ashcan School of early 20th century art.)

Little did the Vanderbilt K's and N's know that they were building their mansions in what was about to become a business district, albeit the world's most exclusive one. Commerce began to make inroads into New York society's most cherished neighborhood just south of 59th Street in the guise of Cartier's, and then The Plaza itself. In 1902, William K. Vanderbilt even sold a lot near his mansion to Morton F. Plant with the provision it remain residential for 25 years — a vain attempt to stem the rising tide of commercialism. Richard McSherry, the grandson of Rollin H. Wilbur, the president of the Lehigh Valley Railroad, told me, "The Vanderbilts, who combined tracts of land on Fifth Avenue the way they did railroads, couldn't stop the onslaught of commercialism which gobbled up their Fifth Avenue holdings."

Jones Harris, son of actress Ruth Gordon and Broadway director-producer Jed Harris, and once married to Heidi Vanderbilt, the granddaughter of Alfred Gwynne Vanderbilt (the first guest to register at The Plaza), says the Vanderbilts and other wealthy families like the Fricks and Carnegies had gravitated to Fifth Avenue because it became the social and domestic hub of "One of the most fortunate pieces of real estate in the world, Manhattan Island. Twenty-third Street used to be 'uptown,' and they kept on going up and up and up. And, of course, all of what we know of northern Manhattan was open country farms, stuff like that. And as you kept going up there was more and more space and you could build bigger and bigger houses . . . . And Fifth Avenue was going to be the dominant Avenue."

It was into this enclave that The Plaza hoped to invite itself — not once but twice, in the form of two elaborate structures. But first a little New York hotel history will help place both Plazas in their very proper context.

New York hotels had already come a long way in the several decades since one urbanologist lamented that New York hostelries lacked the grandeur and stature of their European city counterparts. Financier John Jacob Astor was the first to respond to this civic challenge, calling upon Isaiah Rogers, who had already designed Boston's Tremont House (with eight indoor toilets and eight "bathing rooms"), to design his Astor House, New York City's first real hotel that was more than a boarding house or wayside inn. Located near City Hall Park near Wall Street, the Astor House opened in 1836, and fast became a Mecca of city life of the day.

The Astor House was soon to be eclipsed by the St. Nicholas, built in 1856, "far uptown" on Prince Street, which is now the heart of New York's fashionable *down*town SoHo residential and art gallery district. Aside from rosewood fittings and embroidered drapes, the St. Nicholas boasted a bridal suite complete with "the purest while satin." Even as a new generation of deluxe hotels opened, the 300-room Astor was, fifteen years after it opened in 1836, still the "best hotel in the city," said the *Home Journal*. But by the start of the Civil War the Astor House was supplanted by the grandeur and opulence of the new Fifth Avenue Hotel on Madison Square. Equipped with the city's first passenger elevator and, for the time, an astounding number of "bathing rooms" per floor, the hotel would by many accounts remain the city's premier hotel until the original Plaza opened in 1890 — at a cost of $3 million — and first Waldorf went up three years later.

More than a decade before William Waldorf Astor built the Waldorf at 33rd Street and Fifth Avenue, Fifth Avenue in the 50s was beginning to be heralded not only for the first flush of magnificent family mansions but hotels like The Buckingham, which opened in 1876, fourteen years prior to the original Plaza, on the site of what is now Saks Fifth Avenue at Fifth Avenue and 50th Street.

So, despite the continued carping of critics, New York's hotels were becoming more and more grand, and the further North you got the grander they grew. This trend would eventually culminate with the $12 million "second" Plaza in 1907.

As the 20th Century dawned on Fifth Avenue, commerce would make even further inroads into the domain of the super-rich. The 14-story New Netherland Hotel at 59th Street on the site of the Sherry-Netherland Hotel today, and the old Savoy between 58th and 59th on Fifth, laid claim to the distinction of being Fifth Avenue's northernmost hotel outpost at the time the "new," or second, Plaza was being constructed.

Three blocks south of The Plaza lay The St. Regis, built in 1902 and The Gotham, (nowadays called The Peninsula) on the West Side of Fifth Avenue, which went up three years later in 1905. The Metropolitan Club, which opened in 1894, with its small circular driveway between Fifth and Madison Avenue (more suited for hansom cabs than taxis or cars) and the Gainsborough Studios, completed a year after The Plaza in 1908, and a smattering of nondescript brownstones which have long since been relegated to delis and other use, are the only remaining structures built before 1910 from 58th Street north to 60th Street and from Madison Avenue west to Sixth Avenue.

⌗

Everyone knows sequels are rarely superior to the original, but this was not the case with The Plaza. That "first" Plaza, frankly, was a bit of a bomb. For starters, in the 1880's when construction began, 59th Street or Central Park South, as it later became known, just west of the gilded millionaire-laden Fifth Avenue of the Vanderbilts, was far from being the kind of posh residential street we know today. Brownstones were separated by industrial and building supply shops and ramshackle billboards.

Planned as an apartment hotel much like The Gotham Hotel four blocks to the south on Fifth Avenue, the first Plaza was started in 1883, fully ten years before the original Waldorf would be built at Fifth Avenue and 33rd Street. According to A.M. Stern's *1900*, the old Plaza's builders, Gregory Gilmartin and John Massengale, Phyfe & Campbell, were plagued with financial problems. The fabled New York architecture firm of McKim, Mead and White had to step in to turn the half-finished structure into a neo-Classical-esque luxury hotel.

The first eight-story Plaza resembled somewhat the Italianate design of the shorter six-story Fifth Avenue Hotel. Hotels like The Fifth Avenue and the adjacent Hoffman House had certainly set new New York hotel standards which up to then only the best European hotels embodied. New York's *Real Estate Record* trade newspaper had decried that most New York hotels had "nothing distinctive, nothing metropolitan about them." But the Waldorf and Plaza hotels of the 1890s changed all that.

Kings Handbook said of the design of that doomed first Plaza that it "is one of the most attractive public houses in the wide world, and it represents the highest possibilities attained in constructing and keeping great modern caravansaries . . . and the simple beauty of Italian Renaissance architecture . . . A large part of the main floor is finished with choice marble mosaic pavements, silvered ceilings, exfoliated bronze columns . . . "

You get the idea. But by the middle of the first decade of the new 20th century, this elaborate structure had become outdated. Not to mention the competition it was enduring from the new bevy of hotels listed above. Thus the first Plaza was to fated be replaced, H. W. Frohne wrote in 1907, "by a new one [Plaza] which should be as much superior to its predecessors as the later one was to some of the old down-town establishments of before the war." That's the Civil War, if you're keeping score.

Beinecke, Black, Gates, Hardenbergh and Sterry — the ambitious owners, designers and operators of the new Plaza, more about whom further along — fully expected their "new" hotel to rise from the debris of the old in record time. What they hadn't bargained for is how difficult it would be to dismantle the first Plaza.

The solidity of the early structure was not about to accommodate the new hoteliers. The tips of some pilings, for instance, which had been pummeled into bedrock, had to be dynamited from their sockets. This was in the summer of 1905 and pedestrians sauntering down 59th Street past the Omega Oil billboard ("For Sore Throat and Cold in Chest — Trial Bottle 10¢") looked on in choked amazement at the clouds of smoke accompanying the blasts as this particular "modern caravanserai," itself completed little more than a decade earlier in 1890, was reduced to expensive dust.

Remarkably, despite delays in tearing down the old hotel, the new Plaza was completed two years later, with the George A. Fuller construction company working at breakneck pace. Remember, building construction in that era was more of a hand-made job. The new French Renaissance-style Plaza — its lowest three stories composed of rusticated marble, the rest white glazed brick, all topped by a three-story mansard roof — had an immense amount of detail, exterior as well as interior, to be completed by fine craftsmen. It was an effort closer to constructing a giant stone sculpture than a modern steel-and-glass office building.

The gables and tourelles and balconies which faced both Central Park and Fifth Avenue all had to be chiseled and fashioned by hand. The design team of E. F. Pooley bought the finest linens in Belfast (Irish linens were used at the hotel until 1961), carpets from W. & J. Sloane on 19th Street in Manhattan and 1,650 chandeliers. Everything was meant to recreate a French chateau on a grand New York scale and tapestry, everything except the Oak Room, with its English baronial themed three-story vaulted ceiling and massive wood carvings.

The Commodore's days on The Avenue had ended by 1877. He'd had humble beginnings as a coastal schooner captain and steamboat owner, leading to the grandeur of the family's Newport seaside "cottages." Then the clan assembled the small New York State railroads into the powerful New York Central line. But they were still railroaded out of their midtown manses by the very astounding American commercial vitality they owed their own good fortunes to. However, the spearpoint of that push, The Plaza, would at least become a temporary second home to one Vanderbilt, the Commodore's grandson Alfred Gwynne Vanderbilt. There was also a reminder of the vast Vanderbilt railways down in the new hotel's basement. The Plaza came equipped with its own miniature underground railroad to ferry huge cargoes of coal to the hotel's subterranean boilers via an intricate grid of tracks.

But spectacular new hotels were not the only ones muscling into the Vanderbilts' old neighborhood. In 1907, one million immigrants first set foot on American soil on Ellis Island, the immigrant processing center in New York harbor. Many ended up in the "alphabet cities" of Avenue A, B and C in Lower East Side tenements. Some, however, moved to within a few stones' throws of The Plaza in tenements that cropped up east of Lexington Avenue in the 50s. The top suites at The Plaza were going for $35,000 a year. Tenements could be had for $350 yearly.

The gap between rich and poor at the time was also evident in what people paid for other things. A room at the Brevort Hotel, at Fifth Avenue and 8th Street was $1 a night on the European plan (meals included.) And you could go roundtrip from New York to Niagara Falls for a little more than $10. For years, then, the richness of Fifth Avenue was sandwiched between far humbler neighborhoods to the east and west.

※

This new 18-story Plaza was indeed a skyscraper. Like the new 42-story Waldorf-Astoria when it was built at 50th and Park Avenue in 1931, The Plaza offered unobstructed views of both the East and Hudson Rivers. From the top of its mansard roof you had a wonderful view on clear moonlit nights of the torch of the Statue of Liberty far to the South in New York Harbor.

From the start, The Plaza benefited from The Waldorf's mistakes. For example, every room, with the exception of the servant's rooms on the top floors and various very small rooms scattered around the lower floors, had private baths. And despite its opulence, The Plaza managers took great pains to avoid the public display of overindulgence that was so castigated in the press when the Bradley Martins attempted to capture the glory of the original Versailles for a society function at The Waldorf at the then unheard of price tag of $25,000. So when Bradley's brother, Freddy, who was something in his own time what Elsa Maxwell was to the new Waldorf-Astoria at 50th and Park Avenue a quarter of a century later, "produced" a ball that featured a one-act play called "Mrs. Van Vechetin's Divorce Dance," he relied less on gilt-edge trappings and more on the involvement of society's first ladies.

In one sense, The Plaza and its fabulous suites overlooking Central Park gave the fashionable super-rich, such as the Vanderbilts and Goulds, a chance to expand beyond their townhouses and "try out" apartment style living which was increasingly coming into vogue on Manhattan's West Side at the turn-of-the-century. In the wake of the Dakota apartments success at Central Park West and 72nd Street, many grandiose apartment complexes, such as the Langham, just to the North of the Dakota, the Apthorp, and others rose in all their elegance between 1890 and 1910. Today they are admired as much for their exterior architecture as they are in demand for their interior spaciousness and room configurations.

Fifth Avenue, however, retained most of its single family mansions until the 1920's Manhattan building boom sealed their doom (as well as that of the region's poorer sections) as it did the old Waldorf-Astoria in the increasingly commercial vicinity of 34th Street and Fifth Avenue. The 1920's and 1930's would also see tremendous expansion of luxury hotels, followed by a long period during which new hotel construction would virtually come to a halt. Finally, during the 1990's new hotels such as the limestone-spired Four Seasons on 57th Street near Park Avenue again sprouted anew.

Both The Plaza and the Vanderbilts had been drawn to the otherwise depressed area by the great park, of course. The ultimate urban people's park, Central Park ironically attracted only the best people when it came to those living across the street. It was 843 acres of raw rolling woodlands, climbable cliffs and flatlands, molded and chiseled into a manicured centerpiece for the entire city of New York. The park was drawn from a master plan called the "Greensward Plan," by designers Frederick Law Olmstead and Clavert Vaux nearly half a century before The Plaza was completed. That was at a time when New Yorkers had to take a horse-drawn cab ride or trolley north of the "city" to visit it.

Almost immediately The Park and The Plaza were intertwined, with Plaza guests both frolicking in and enjoying the view of the perfectly spaced trees, graceful arched stone bridges and even the carousel or, more accurately, carousels. The park's current carousel, which features 58 painted wooden horses and is the fourth to twirl on the same site at 64th Street near Central Park West since 1870, was originally built in 1908, hand-crafted by the Brooklyn firm of Stein and Goldstein.

Moreover, the "grand promenade" near the Mall between

66th and 69th Street on the east side of the park was envisioned by its designers as a kind of outdoor "Peacock Alley." (The original Peacock Alley was a gilded corridor that linked the old Waldorf built in 1893, and its "new" Astoria addition, built in 1897.) Some of The Plaza's fashionable new guests could strut in their latest finery from the wide gilded Peacock Alley-like corridors of the first two floors of The Plaza, past a small lake, over a few gentle rolling hills, onto the Mall.

Albert Pasteur's *The Elegant Inn*, about the original Waldorf on Fifth Avenue between 33rd and 34th Streets, explains how all those many new hotels including The Astor in Times Square and The Knickerbocker at 42nd Street, The St. Regis at 55th Street, and The Gotham across the avenue, began slowly to siphon guests from The Waldorf.

"But the old Waldorf Astoria's most formidable competition," writes the author, "proved to be The Plaza, which came along in the fall of 1907 at Fifth Avenue's southeast entrance to Central Park."

The Plaza drained ideas as well as guests from the Fifth Avenue and 34th Street establishment.

Besides raiding the Waldorf-Astoria's famous guest list, The Plaza also borrowed the names of some of its famous rooms. There was an Oak Room at the old Waldorf long before there was one at The Plaza.

Karl Schriftgiesser wrote in *Oscar of the Waldorf* (about Oscar Tschirey, a legendary maitre d') of the Oak Room's place in New York and Waldorf history: "So many of the old houses were coming down in the year 1897 [the year the Astoria addition was built] and so many people of prominence were moving uptown, that the Waldorf naturally became the rallying point of Society. . . . The living and dining facilities of the hotel were taxed; many a would-be guest was turned away. Debutante parties were now being given in the hotel instead of in private homes. The Oak Room, where huge pine logs burned slowly all day and night in great fireplaces, was the most popular rendezvous. People came to sit, to smoke, to talk, to read and write — and to be seen."

With the perhaps notable exception of the huge roasting pine logs, much of that tradition would continue at The Plaza's Oak Room. It had opened in 1912, was closed five years later when Prohibition was enacted, then in 1944, under Hilton, was reopened as a bar and light-dining spot.

⋇

But this new splendid structure called The Plaza — named, incidentally, after a broad, paved cab-turnaround in front of it, and since transformed into Pulitzer Fountain and Grand Army Plaza — had sprung as much from beefsteak as from high society.

Bernhard ("Ben") Beinecke, a poor German immigrant who'd eventually come to own a massive stockyard at 59th Street and the Hudson River, had dreams not of sugar plums but of hotels. The erstwhile stocky, gregarious butcher-wagon driver wanted to build an exclusive enclave for his increasingly exclusive and fabulously rich friends. He got together with Canadian-born Henry S. Black, president of the George A. Fuller (construction) Company, and the two entrepreneurs cooked up the idea for the new Plaza. Eve Brown, the former publicist for The Plaza, relates in her book *The Plaza* that Beinecke, Black and their associates were having lunch at The St. Regis discussing where to get the financing for their dream hotel when a voice from another table bellowed: "Get Fred Sterry to manage the hotel and you can count on me for all you need! I'll wager a fortune on his hotel ability."

Hotelier Fred Sterry was renowned at the time for his running of the Homestead in Hot Springs, Virginia, but the booming voice belonged to none other than Wall Street financier John "Bet-a-Million" Gates. He would go on to raise a lot of the unprecedented $12 million cost to construct The Plaza. Even though, as it happened, it wasn't the best of times to be doing so.

The very early 1900's had seen unparalleled prosperity as railroads, oil, steel and other monopolies ballooned in power and influence, but by 1907, as the front doors of The Plaza were about to swing open, the American economy suddenly stumbled into recession. The stock market crashed and President Teddy Roosevelt's relentless trust-busting caused sleepless nights for even the craftiest robber barons.

Black made it through that depression but would kill himself with a single shot in July 1930, during the first fallout from the 1929 crash of the stock market. (By the teens, more Plaza builders were dying. Bet-a-Million Gates died in 1911 leaving an estate valued at the time at $30 to $40 million. Architect Hardenbergh, born in 1847, died seven years later on May 13, 1918.)

Frederick Sterry, on the other hand, born in Lansingburg in upstate New York, became the dominant force at The Plaza from the time it opened in 1907 almost until his death at age 67 in 1933. Sterry began his hotel career at the Grand Union Hotel in Saratoga Springs, New Lakewood, New Jersey, then in 1893 became manager of the Homestead, propelling it to the front ranks of America's greatest establishments.

Beginning in 1905, Sterry worked with John Gates, Bernhard Beinecke and the builders and architects of The Plaza to plan the interior and running of the grand hotel. In 1907, when The Plaza opened in October of that year, Sterry was appointed the hotel's managing director. He eventually was able to expand the empire of his hotel influence by becoming a vice-president of the Copley Plaza in Boston, built in 1912, and The Greenbrier, rebuilt in 1913.

William Beinecke, grandson of Bernhard Beinecke, turned 86 on May 22, 2000. He confided to me one of his very earliest memories, from when he was just five years old, in 1919, of seeing a parade down Fifth Avenue out the window of his grandfather's Plaza suite.

"Think of this!" Beinecke began. "My grandfather came in a

sailing vessel to New York in 1865 and in 1907 — less than 40 years later — he was the entrepreneur who opened The Plaza Hotel, which in 1907 standing at 59th Street and Fifth Avenue was something! I was living out in New Jersey and my parents brought me in to see a parade from my grandfather's suite. I can barely remember looking out the windows of The Plaza Hotel on the 12th floor on the Fifth Avenue side. After my grandfather died, my family still owned the hotel and my father and my uncle sold it to Conrad Hilton in the 1940's."

"I didn't have any idea of the extent of the Beinecke family's equity interest in The Plaza until much later. But the hotel was familiar territory to me from the time I was quite small, and I was at home there." writes Beinecke is his book *Through Memory's Haze*. "So, too, were my other Beinecke cousins who were about my age; in fact it is alleged that my cousin Betsy was the model for the heroine of Kay Thompson's popular children's book *Eloise* [many more candidates for this not necessarily flattering distinction to follow]. Certainly long before the *Eloise* series came into being, Betsy was rampaging through the hallways, teasing the doorman, running the elevators up and down. I was more interested in the elevators themselves. They were the old-fashioned plunger types that have long since been replaced by cable-suspended ones. The plunger elevators were hydraulically driven and rested on columns, and when the cars went down, those columns descended into the earth . . ."

Beinecke also tells the story in his book about a 6'4" Plaza doorman named Ralph, who had a twin brother at The Pierre, (and the same height) and Ralph would put drunks into a cab and send them to The Pierre. "It was a source of amazement to a considerable number of high-class New York drunks that the big man who put them into a cab at The Plaza was there to help them out of it at The Pierre!" Beinecke writes.

In 1922, Sterry further exercised his hold on The Plaza when he was elected president of The Plaza Operating Company, succeeding Bernhard Beinecke, who became chairman of the board. Two years later Sterry announced a reorganization plan which permitted him to take full charge of the famed Fifth Avenue Hotel, assuming practically all managing duties.

Sterry is credited with building the addition to The Plaza as well as luring the rich and famous of the day to live permanently at the hotel. "The wide popularity and untiring energy of Mr. Sterry were to a large extent responsible for the growth of the hotel's patronage to an extent that required the building of (some 300) additional rooms," the trade publication *Hotel Review* reported in April, 1924.

Ironically, just as The Plaza had radically changed the landscape of Fifth Avenue and Central Park South at the beginning of the century, the continuing development of the area as a business as well as a hotel and recreational center would raise eyebrows at what became the old guard Plaza half a century later. When the 52-story General Motors Building was going up in the late 1960s Plaza general manager Arthur Dooley feared the area was indeed taking a turn for the worse. To his surprise and pleasure the GM Building was "set back" sufficiently from Fifth Avenue by virtue of its own mini-plaza. A highly relieved Dooley was able to proclaim there was "even greater open space in front of The Plaza" in 1967 with the addition of the skyscraper than there had been with the much shorter old Savoy Plaza Hotel. Dooley and The Plaza had certainly lucked out better than the Vanderbilts and their mansions forty years earlier.

The Art of Design, and of Living, at The Plaza

Long before the great hotel could be filled or even built on the precisely 53,726 square feet of choice real estate available to it, it had to be designed. And for that job The Plaza's high-rolling entrepreneurs had enlisted the talents of one of the best.

Henry Hardenbergh's legacy was first founded on his design for the Dakota Apartments at 72nd Street and Central Park West, erected in 1884. Two decades later his plan for The Plaza would forever cement that reputation.

After the Dakota, Hardenbergh further developed his art with the Manhattan Hotel at Madison Avenue and 43rd Street, in the hub of majestic "railroad hotels." In the immediate vicinity of Grand Central Terminal, these included not only the Manhattan and The Biltmore, but The Commodore, and much further south but connected by its own private railroad spur, The Vanderbilt Hotel at 34th Street and Park Avenue.

According to *1900*, Hardenbergh "did not abandon the chateauesque domesticity of his earlier work, but the overall composition and detailing of The Plaza Hotel were far more disciplined and ordered than at the Waldorf-Astoria. The details of The Plaza hinted at the style of Francois I, but they were deliberately restrained and concentrated at the mansard roof where the filigree softened the skyline silhouette. The simple mass below presented Hardenbergh's clearest statement of the tripartite skyscraper formula, with a rusticated limestone base alluding to traditional masonry construction and unarticulated shaft sheathed in terra cotta. The result was a masterful combination of *gemuetlichkeit* and classical rigor."

Ten years before The Plaza, Hardenbergh had designed The Hotel Manhattan in 1883. Other New York work included the Astoria addition to The Waldorf. The latter was deemed a major improvement both in terms of architectural flourishes on the outside and the use of space on the inside.

In the *Times* in 1982, architecture critic Paul Goldberger wrote that Hardenbergh's "great gift was in the manipulation of historic detail in such a way as to create elegant, strong compositions that served not only interior needs, but also the complex demands of the New York cityscape. His buildings were never just objects in themselves — in other words they were, and continue to be, pieces of the city that related to everything that is around them.

"The Plaza, for example, is a building that both faces a special open space, Grand Army Plaza, and anchors the eastern end of Central Park South . . . [It is] lively enough to be a vibrant edge for the park, and still, with all of this, domestic enough in feelings to be a proper hotel.

"The inside reflects Hardenbergh's priorities. The rooms are grand in scale and yet relatively simple in detail; for all their reliance on historical elements, they have never been fussy or prissy."

Which is perhaps what led Frank Lloyd Wright, a notorious opponent of both historicist architecture in general and of any building not from his own hand, to suspend his prejudices, and declare The Plaza his favorite hotel. In fact, he maintained a second floor corner suite (223-225) there from 1953, when construction started on the Wright-designed Guggenheim Museum, to his death in 1959. Called "Taliesin East," a reference to the school he designed dubbed "Taliesin West" in

Arizona, Wright filled the red and purple suite with his own austere tables and chairs and a drafting table. It was dismantled after his death but Ivana and Donald Trump, in an astute PR move, recreated it in 1989 with Wright reproductions and named it the Frank Lloyd Wright Suite.

In 1973, a guidebook critic lauded the timelessness of The Plaza's architecture: "I like these vast beautiful hotels which have nothing modern about them but have acquired pasts thanks to their rich decoration. There are living pasts and dead pasts. The Plaza reflects a past of simple, moneyed times."

Hardenbergh's grandest hotel does get mixed reviews from some sources. Renowned architect I. M. Pei, who designed the ultra modern new wing at the Louvre in Paris, the mammoth and the equally modern Christian Science Center in Boston, told me he believes, "The architecture of The Plaza is nothing special. It's of that period. It belongs to that particular period 1905, 1906. And I wouldn't consider it a masterpiece . . . Many of our greatest buildings have been torn down. That's unfortunate. The Morgan Library is a very nice building and I would say the Frick House [on Fifth Avenue and 70th Street] is, another," Pei added. "The Knickerbocker Club [at Fifth Avenue and 62nd Street] is a beautiful building. But many are overwhelmed by the new."

Architecture historian Christopher Gray lauds Hardenbergh's contribution to the city's landscape. "Even though many of his other buildings have been demolished, Henry Janeway Hardenbergh left an indelible legacy to New York City," Gray wrote in the *Times* in May, 2000. "In the early 1900's Hardenbergh got four plum hotel commissions — The Willard in Washington (1902), The Plaza (1907), The Martinique at 32nd Street and Broadway (1910) and Boston's Copley Plaza (1912) — that firmly established him as a specialist in steel-frame hotel design."

Hardenbergh, with the aid of Frederick Sterry and the financial backing of John "Bet-a-Million" Gates, equipped his most successful architectural creation, his "chateau skyscraper," as it was also called, with the accouterments of a late 19th century townhouse lavish enough even for the Vanderbilts.

⌗

From the very first day, The Plaza became home to the world's most extravagant people — some extravagant in wealth or social position, some extravagant in more mercurial ways.

Clara Bell Walsh, a Kentucky debutante, first set foot in The Plaza on October 1, 1907, and never lived anywhere else until she was carried out the front door to a funeral home on August 2, 1957. Mrs. Walsh didn't limit her acquaintances and friends to society and Broadway. An ardent horsewoman, she was also an early champion, in her own personal way, of human rights, inviting prominent blacks into her apartment at a time they were barred even from entertaining downstairs. One of her best friends was Bill ("Bojangles") Robinson, the black tap dancer who rocketed to international fame. Nevertheless, his renown didn't shield him from the racial profiling of his day. A security guard spotted him coming off the elevator on Walsh's floor one time and immediately asked the entertainer what he was doing there. Whereupon Bojangles literally danced his explanation that he was visiting his friend Mrs. Walsh. Which was all the dumbfounded guard needed to know.

'When I met her in the 1940s she was a rather large, imposing woman," recollects Joan Marlowe Rahe, a former Broadway actress and theatrical publisher (*The Theater Information Bulletin* and *Theatre Critics' Reviews*) who also happens to be my mother. She resided with my father in a one-bedroom suite at The Plaza in the early 1940s about the time he was writing that biography of George M. Cohan.

"She liked," my mother continued about Mrs. Walsh, "to go to the theater and she'd invite me down to her suite — I don't remember much but it had a large living room — and we had a drink before we went to the theater. She was an older woman when I knew her and that was in the early 1940s."

Mr. and Mrs. Cornelius K. G. Billings, whose country home once stood on the spot where the fabulous Cloisters Museum stands today, joined Mrs. Walsh on that fateful first day. There was also John Gates, and his wife and son, and Mr. and Mrs. Gould. Mrs. Gould, the former Edith Kingdom had married a millionaire in Mr. George J. Gould (layabout socialite son of the infamous, occasional Vanderbilt rival Jay Gould, a man once dubbed by a Pulitzer newspaper as, "one of the most sinister figures that ever flitted bat-like across the vision of the American people"), then retired from the professional stage to enter the loftier theatre of New York high society. Years later, another Plaza habitué, actress Irene Purcell, would also marry very well and retire. She wed an heir of the Johnson's Wax fortune.

And when John "Bet-a-Million" Gates, who helped finance The Plaza's construction, left his aerie at The Waldorf-Astoria for a huge suite of sixteen rooms at The Plaza that first crisp October day in 1907, it announced a change in the old order. "New York" had once again shifted uptown.

Another of the new residents at The Plaza was Lord Duveen, who sold art to financiers like Andrew Mellon and others of his ilk. Alfred Gwynne Vanderbilt, that very first hotel guest, had parents living in the Vanderbilt mansion, a stone's throw from The Plaza on 58th Street. Was he checking into the rival accommodations across the street as some sort of youthful rebellion? No, it was a carefully orchestrated public relations move by The Plaza's owners.

"My grandfather had a suite of nine rooms on the northeast corner of the hotel and it rented for $25,000 a year," explains Vanderbilt's grandson, Alfred Vanderbilt, Jr. It was at The Plaza about a year later that Alfred Gwynne Vanderbilt met and married Harriet Emerson, the daughter of the inventor of Bromo Selzer. And while Alfred Gwynne Vanderbilt could take no credit for building The Plaza, Vanderbilt Jr. notes, "It was the groundbreaking residential hotel of the age and my grandfather went on to build The Vanderbilt Hotel at 34th Street and

Park Avenue and The Commodore," (after Commodore Vanderbilt) which has long since been remodeled to become New York's Grand Hyatt Hotel.

"It was a great public relations coup to get my grandfather to live at the hotel," his grandson explains. Alfred's life took a couple of strange turns, good and bad, afterward, however. A few years later, he would book passage on the ill-fated *Titanic* in 1912 but changed his plans before it sailed from Southampton. His lifelong good luck finally ran out when he went down with the *Lusitania*.

Charles Melville Hays, who was General Manager of the Grand Trunk Railway (which was purchased by Canadian National Railways in 1919 and Canadian Pacific in 1988) ran out of his good fortune when he, unlike Mr. Vanderbilt, was booked to stay at The Plaza and did not forego his passage on the *Titanic*. Also on board ship was — and presumably still is — the custom furniture he planned to install in the Chateau Frontenac in Quebec after his stay at The Plaza.

If Alfred Gwynne Vanderbilt's death aboard the *Lusitania* in May 1915 wasn't enough of a personal loss in the fallout of World War I, Germany's diplomatic staff stationed in New York and Washington, D.C., and which was unceremoniously ordered to sail from New York back to the Fatherland in February 1917, were among some of The Plaza's most ardent early patrons. But with anti-Germany sentiment running so high manager Sterry was relieved that these guests, including Countess von Bernstorff, wife of the German Ambassador to the United States, was spared any possible indignities that might arise even from his well-trained staff. It would have been doubly hard for many of the bellboys and clerks who cheered speeches made right outside the hotel in Grand Army Plaza by the likes of silent screen goddess Mary Pickford against Germany to treat von Berstorff and others with the same respect with which they had been accustomed over the years.

Nevertheless, though a long way from the terrible trenches of the Western Front, their horrors were brought home to some of The Plaza's residents in deeply moving personal terms. Clara Bell Walsh, for instance, was mystified when a women asked her to help her find some striped trousers and a mourning coat. "My son died yesterday and is being buried tomorrow," the grief stricken woman told Walsh. "And so many of his friends are sick with the flu I can't find enough pallbearers." Walsh found the trousers and coat and attended the young man's funeral herself.

Also in line to register that first day were Mr. and Mrs. William (Win) G. Roelker of Newport, then "Diamond Jim" Brady, Mr. and Mrs. George Jay Gould, Mr. and Mrs. Oliver Harriman (the railroad magnate) and John Wanamaker of Philadelphia and clothing-store fame.

Wanamaker lived at The Plaza five days a week, then went to his country estate on weekends. But his love of nature was such that after long early morning walks in Central Park he would regale Plaza doormen with his sightings of birds and squirrels.

Six weeks after that first parade of wealth and privilege registered, the hotel suffered its first major scandal. Although a tempest in a teapot by today's cable-network standards, a Mrs. Campbell, a renowned English actress, had the utter audacity, the overwhelming cheek, to actually light up a cigarette within the public confines of the establishment. Lucius Boomer — later president of The Waldorf-Astoria — rushed in to try to put out the fire, so to speak. But Mrs. Campbell would have none of it.

"I have been given reason to understand this is a free country," she answered Boomer's entreaties. "I propose to do nothing to alter its status." However, now that she had made her point — and the headlines of the next day's papers — she extinguished her cigarette and departed the defiled premises.

Long before the Prince of Wales gave up the English throne for an American commoner, Wallis Warfield Simpson, "the woman I love," and lived at The Waldorf Towers whenever he came to New York, the Prince stayed at The Plaza. And as he did at The Waldorf Towers, the Prince seemed happiest not at big society bashes where people paid insincere homage to his station but talking to rank-and-file Plaza employees like bell-men and cooks. Still, whenever the Prince was in the hotel it was an occasion for celebration and once, a little to his majesty's embarrassment, a Plaza chef grilled some extra thin pancakes, or crepes, and smothered them in sweet sauce and asked what the Prince would like to call the new creation. He said "Suzette," after his date, whose identity has been a mystery over years.

The oft-married American actress Lillian Russell, who became a household name in the 1890s for her delightful performances as "Lady Teazie" and other musical comedies of the day, was frequently a luncheon guest of Diamond Jim Brady at The Plaza. But she didn't come alone. She wheeled up to the hotel's Central Park South steps on her diamond-studded bicycle which a few years earlier had helped her shed nearly 30 pounds of her ample girth. She usually left her bejeweled bicycle with the doorman, who put it behind lock and key in a luggage room to the right of the 59th Street entrance.

The hotel's porters were both in awe of the bejeweled bike and terrified someone might steal it. Thickly gold-plated and covered with diamonds, it was valued at $10,000, a small fortune in those days and nearly half of what Alfred Gwynne Vanderbilt paid for his enormous Plaza suite that first year of operation.

Miss Russell and Mr. Brady, oblivious to the porters' trepidations, would then proceed to the Terrace Room, where the hotel's Fifth Avenue entrance is now. When not dining, Russell took long, long rides in Central Park, up around the Reservoir beginning at its southern tip just above 86th Street, up along its northern rim and then west around what's now called the Sheep Meadow.

Although they were never married, Russell would often stay at Brady's ornate brownstone on West 86th Street, where he kept a spare bedroom for her. It's also likely they spent time alone together at The Plaza after "Diamond Jim" brought her "a little doodad," as he termed the diamond-encrusted pins he picked up (mostly in pawn shops) on his many travels. We'll never know for sure about their stays because of The Plaza's steely, longstanding reputation for tightlippedness. Generally, a guest's secrets are safer with the staff than his or her valuables are in the hotel vault. Yet another way to insure repeat business with the well-to-do.

Perhaps the most unusual aristocrat ever to move in as "a permanent" at the hotel was Princess Vilma Lwoff-Parlaghy, who lived there until World War I. The Princess, whose suite of rooms came equipped with a whopping price tag of $1,333 a month, "swept," writes Eve Brown, "into The Plaza accompanied by a retinue consisting of a royal surgeon, a private secretary, a chamberlain resplendent in blue military coat with gold epaulets."

She also famously brought along a few favorite pets, among them a lion cub she'd sweet-talked Ringling Brothers into selling her. Named "Goldfleck" by the princess, the cub severely tested the famous tolerance of the hotel's staff. But some things are too much even for The Plaza to accommodate. Not that the feline was evicted outright. Managing Director Fred Sterry requested that Goldfleck check in with a full-time trainer. A brilliant solution, since the hotel instead of alienating one guest, gained another.

The Plaza, like The Waldorf-Astoria, prided (no lion pun intended) itself on its open door pets policy. In the 1950s there were some 35 dogs living at The Plaza and some of the bellboy staff were regularly dispatched for dog runs in Central Park.

One animal superstar, Roy Rogers' horse Trigger, purported to have stayed at The Plaza in the 1950's probably didn't actually sleep there, Roy's son Dusty Rogers told me. "Dad used to give horses to the mounted police when he'd come to town for rodeos and wherever dad went Trigger was there, in the lobbies of theaters, in hotel lobbies, stores. He had special rubber shoes so his trusty mount wouldn't slip. So while

Trigger was at The Plaza [probably for a press conference Roy had there] dad kept him at the Garden (Madison Square Garden) and he either spent the night at the Garden or maybe in a trailer outside parked outside The Plaza."

Publicist Lee Solters, who signed a $2000 a month contract ("plus expenses") in 1971 to represent The Plaza, once enlisted Ringling Brothers Circus to drum up publicity. He pre-registered a guest named "Miss Ella Phant," and no one at the front desk thought twice of it until Solters showed up at the 59th Street entrance of the hotel with a baby elephant and a swarm of reporters. At first an irate front desk clerk, who was not briefed about the gag, refused to register Miss Phant. Solters clued him in under his breath and Miss Phant, who while she weighed several hundred pounds still could get into an elevator cab, was ushered upstairs — and then out the service elevator.

Which brings to mind the most well-trained pet that ever lived at The Plaza — a Boston bulldog owned by a Mrs. Benjamin B. Kirkland of Philadelphia who lived in the hotel in 1908. Every evening "Captain," the bulldog, left the area of the hotel safe (where the safe-deposit boxes are now next to the front desk) holding a Russian leather jewel case between his teeth and, followed obediently by Mrs. Kirkland's maid, waddled into a waiting elevator cab. From there he went straight to Mrs. Kirkland's suite with the maid in tow. The jewels in the leather case were said to be worth several hundred thousand dollars and despite the relative gentility of the times, Plaza manager Sterry asked that a Pinkerton security guard occasionally follow the maid who was following her "Captain."

Born in Hungary in 1865, Princess Vilma Lwoff-Parlaghy had married a Russian prince but had divorced him by the time she came to the United States. She studied painting in Munich under Franz von Lentabach and in America painted portraits of Thomas Edison, August Belmont, and Andrew Carnegie. While at The Plaza, the Princess reportedly got $15,000 per portrait, but her extravagant life-style vastly exceeded any earned income.

When her fortune was wiped out by the revolution in Russia, she moved from The Plaza to a townhouse at 109 East 39th Street. She would prove just one of a long line of artists, actors, and writers who would bestow upon The Plaza a reputation as a kind of gilded cage for gifted eccentrics.

Here, in no particular time or other order are a few more of the hotel's "characters":

One of the most fabulous Plaza eccentrics in recent years was the late Princess Audrey who came to the Palm Court night after night with her husband Prince Robert. Living just a few doors from The Plaza on Central Park South, The Princess wore huge elaborately festooned mink coats even on the hottest summer nights. A strict vegetarian, she scorned red meat and chicken and even fish and brought some of her own fixings to the Palm Court, including a small jar of peanut butter she spread generously on white or whole wheat toast. Rumor had it that she was a Mercedes Benz or another European auto heiress. She had married a real prince, who had a title and lived mostly on his wits and engaging personality. When Audrey got older she became incontinent at times and wasn't welcomed as she had been for years at The Palm Court. When she died in early 2000, a good friend, New York actress Annette Hunt, had a memorial party for her in the Palm Court "It was where she always belonged even after she was buried!" Hunt remarked.

"Then, too, there was the unfortunate episode of Baron Richard Von Arkovy," writes Lucius Beebe. "The Baron lived up to the most exacting standards required by the press of visiting nobility in that he was never seen without formal evening attire and, in addition to a gold headed walking stick and astrakhan overcoat, constantly sported a silk top hat and single eyeglass. There was considerable flurry when the Baron was arrested in the Oak Room on a charge of grand larceny, having it was stated, purloined a collection of jewelry from the Chancellor of the Cuban Government. Interest in the Baron's attire rose to fever heat when the police discovered that, as a complement to his other accouterments, he carried what the *Tribune* described as 'a set of Apache knuckles adorned with heavy spikes,' which no gentleman would be without."

But not all of the outlandish Plaza characters were guests. Some were employed there. Tall, handsome, ramrod straight, with Basil Rathbone-like movie star gaunt good looks, Serge Obolensky's talent for organizing glittering parties was never more in evidence than during his Plaza celebrations of the Russian Orthodox Christmas every January 6 and the Russian Easter. Versailles may not have had as many floral decorations. But it was his creation of The Plaza's Rendez Vous Room in a space once occupied by the Grill Room of the roaring twenties and F. Scott Fitzgerald's era that put him in a pantheon of hotel notables that included Lucius Boomer and Elsa Maxwell of The Waldorf-Astoria and Freddy Martin of The Plaza. Just two years after it opened in 1947 the Rendez Vous Room was grossing a half-million dollars, a princely sum for any nightclub of the era. But the most permanent thing Obolensky left The Plaza was commissioning five chandeliers which were copies of those that hung in the Palace of Pallovsky in St. Petersburg where they had been shipped from Versailles after the French Revolution at then fire-sale prices. The copies were actually fashioned by Charles Winston, the brother of famed jeweler Harry Winston.

Obolensky was among a long list of immigrants from Czarist Russia to rise to power at The Plaza. Oblensky's royal heritage and bearing served royalty well and nonroyals royally. He also distinguished himself in the U.S. Army during World War II, after which Colonel Obolensky was joined at The Plaza by another fellow countryman, Vasilli Adlerberg, who became an assistant manager. Both men had to swallow some of their national pride in mother Russia when Soviet Ambassador to the United Nations Andrei A. Gromyko and his entourage arrived at The Plaza for an extended stay while their consulate quarters were under construction. Yet aside from being at odds politically, Obolensky and Gromyko had many things in common, including their love of caviar. But even Obolensky was shocked to hear that the ambassador and his staff had a standing order for 100 pounds of the finest Russian beluga caviar to be delivered to the hotel every month. "What does he do with it, sell it?" Obolensky was heard telling colleagues jokingly.

Freddy Martin of The Plaza was, just to name a few endeavors, major domo, social director, hotel promoter, gadfly and discreet go between for the highly public personality and the private illicit affair. Freddy was on a first name basis with kings and potentates, pimps and prostitutes. In short, Freddy had the knack of "introducing people" although he didn't keep his hand out, according to one Plaza source (unlike The Waldorf's similar social "arranger" Elsa Maxwell). He loved people and was never happier then when two people he had introduced clicked.

Like Elsa Maxwell's barnyard balls at The Waldorf-Astoria, complete with real cows and chickens on beds of real hay, Martin also became famous for his annual Bowery Mission Ball benefiting Bowery derelicts. As quick-witted and sharp-tongued as Maxwell was years later, Martin managed to offend both his tony benefactors and some of the bums he had taken under his society wings with his proclamation that, "Where idleness and extravagance creep in, decay begins."

※

In its early history, when The Plaza enjoyed a veritable flood of society, the ballroom was in constant employ, and in particular for those amateur theatricals the rich so relished and could so easily afford to mount. This, however, posed a serious construction question to the hotel's owners — how to build a stage in their one ballroom seemed an insurmountable obstacle.

Finally, Otis Elevator came up with the idea for one entire side of the ballroom's ornate balcony to be turned into an elevator, which, like Radio City Music Hall's stage many years later, would be raised or lowered at the push of a button. The stage became The Plaza's own counterpart of the Amateur Comedy Club, where young women and aging society doyennes were cast in various amateur theatrics.

One reproduction — the word reproduction is apt because they weren't full-fledged plays — was called "Mrs. Van Veehten's Divorce Dance," and starred socialite Mrs. George Gould, who lived at the hotel with her financier husband. "The setting and costuming of the private theatricals is often the professional's admiration and despair, for no expense is spared and no triumph of the artist's creation is beyond their reach," *Theater Magazine* sniffily reported.

A few years down the pike, in an effort to accommodate the growing post World War I Jazz Age popularity of The Plaza, a 300-room addition was built in 1921 on the 58th Street side of the grand hotel nearest the Vanderbilt mansion. Topped by a cavernous presidential suite that was perched high enough to peer over the north wall of the hotel (its 59th Street, Central Park side), the addition gradually became the bastion of many of the hotel's permanent residents, including bandleader Eddie Duchin, chanteuse Hildegarde, and various and sundry expatriate East European royals.

The addition featured a whole new grand ballroom to accommodate the ongoing social crush, and which today remains a favorite of society, the media, and the entertainment industries. At the time, however, it changed the hotel's main entrance from 59th Street to Fifth Avenue and Pulitzer Fountain, where limousines have streamed by ever since and where, less frequently, the rich and famous like those most famous of Twenties scamps F. Scott and Zelda Fitzgerald have frolicked in the waters fully clothed.

By the 1950s the number of "permanents" would dwindle from close to 90 percent when the hotel opened in 1907 down to some 20 percent. (Even as late as 1971, the permanents, included celebrities like opera diva Maria Callas, TV personality David Frost, movie mogul Darryl Zanuck and *Eloise* creator

EARLY PLAZA ADVERTISING FOR THE LONG SINCE DEPARTED PLAZA TERRACE

FORMER PLAZA EXEC JEFFREY FLOWERS, AN FAO SCHWARTZ REPRESENTATIVE, AND STUFFED FRIENDS POSE BEFORE THE SECOND ELOISE PORTRAIT — THE FIRST WAS SNITCHED MYSTERIOUSLY IN 1960

MY FATHER WARD MOREHOUSE, LEFT, SEATED NEXT TO MY MOTHER, JOAN MARLOWE RAHE, LIVING THE CAFE LIFE

MY STEPMOTHER, REBECCA MOREHOUSE, WITH ACTRESS ETHEL BARRYMORE

THE PULITZER FOUNTAIN ON FIFTH AVENUE, FEATURING POMONA, ROMAN
GODDESS OF ABUNDANCE

Kay Thompson.) At the same time, the number of transient stars staying at The Plaza continued to soar. In August 1953, for example, Greer Garson, Cary Grant, Stewart Granger and Zsa Zsa Gabor were registered; the following month Orson Welles, Norman Rockwell and ballet star Margot Fonteyn, had checked in.

The following decade would bring The Beatles and Liz Taylor and Richard Burton to the hotel. But the "biggest" celebrity to pass through The Plaza's doors was the 4000-pound outrigger canoe from the Marlon Brando remake of *Mutiny on the Bounty*, installed in Trader Vic's when it opened in an area once occupied by a barbershop and steam room.

Over the decades, the styles and lifestyles of the hotel's glittering guests would change — and change the hotel itself. One thing that has never altered, however, is the hotel's dedication to hospitality. There is no better example of this than little Eddie Murphy.

You see, long before there was an Eddie Murphy film star there was an Eddie Murphy Plaza star. The latter Murphy was a 10-year old kid who lived in a tenement several blocks from The Plaza on East 62nd Street. It was back in the winter of 1910 and he was out skating on the pond in front of The Plaza in Central Park when he accidentally fell through the ice. He was fished out by the chauffeur of a Plaza dowager who happened to be walking by the pond, given a hot bath and new suit of clothes and a hearty hot meal. Little Eddie said he couldn't wait to tell "da gang" on East 62nd Street about his bath at Da Plaza.

A Virtual Tour of The Plaza

The Pulitzer Fountain, with Karl Bitter's statue of Pomona, the Roman goddess of abundance, was installed in 1916, five years after newspaper czar Joseph Pulitzer bequeathed $50,000 for a memorial in his name at his death. In 1913, Carrere & Hastings, the architecture firm which designed the fountain, won a competition in which the layout of the fountain reflected the symmetry of Saint-Gaudens' statue of General Sherman a block north. It is now for many the first public "stop" on one's way into the Fifth Avenue entrance of The Plaza, under the somewhat obscured grandeur of the back-to-back-P Tiffany window ensconced above the wide awning.

But let's now travel back, briefly, "virtually," to a crisp autumn afternoon and pretend you're standing on the southern fringe of Central Park, with no Pomona, no General Sherman, just a broad cab "turnaround" plaza spread out before a giant, brand-new hotel.

You're Alfred Gwynne Vanderbilt and friends have recommended that you move from your family's home on the corner of 58th Street and Fifth Avenue to the magnificent new 18-story Plaza Hotel between your home and the park. Never in the history of New York has there been so much hoopla in the press about the opening of a hotel and hundreds stand ten and twelve people deep craning their necks to get a glimpse of the rich and famous checking into the skyscraper hotel destined to dominate midtown Manhattan like no other structure before it, and, to a great extent, after it. (A towering forest of glass and steel office skyscrapers has since sprouted up all around the hotel, but none has overshadowed it, architecturally or culturally.)

The prices of those first suites averaged, on a yearly rental basis, from $15,000 to $35,000 in a hotel that had more than 100 suites and 200 single rooms. And while this was an enormous sum at a time when some construction workers were lucky to earn a few dollars a day, "The prices paid are not really in excess of what it would cost to maintain a Fifth Avenue home," the Philadelphia *North American* reported.

It's interesting to note the enormous number of connecting rooms that the first guests to register at The Plaza took, a tradition that has, more or less, continued with the King of Morocco as well as with Saudi Arabia Prince Alwaleed Bin Talal, co-owner of The Plaza, and even Michael Douglas and Catherine Zeta-Jones on their honeymoon. For example, of these first guests, Mr. and Mrs. Vanderbilt "and servant" were assigned a total of nine rooms, 521 through 529; the William G. Roelkers "and maid" got rooms 1141 through 1145; and the Young-Heyworths were ushered to 237-245.

As Vanderbilt and Roelker settled into to their sumptuous quarters, general manager Sterry escorted a phalanx of press on a tour of the world's grandest hotel. The New York *World* newspaper raved: "The great 18-story building was light from top to bottom. But the exterior gave only a faint hint of the glorious interior marble and gold and wonderful tapestries which vied with each other at dazzling the sight, in thousands of electric lights."

Maids and manservants of the rich and famous who lived at The Plaza, by the way, stayed in small rooms in the topmost tower sections of the hotel like they once did at The Dakota, also designed by Plaza architect Hardenbergh.

That first October night in 1907 guests would have dined on Poulet Saute for $1.50 or Terrapin, Baltimore for $3.50. For desert, there was "Vanille" ice cream for 30 cents or Tutti-Frutti for 40 cents.

Let's clean up one legendary misconception before proceeding with this virtual tour. Although the Fifth Avenue entrance of The Plaza is what most people think of as the main entrance of the hotel, the grander Central Park South one always was the front entrance. "This was always the front entrance," says Jeffrey Jacobs, the hotel's food and beverage director who will serve as a guide on the first leg of our tour. "Fifth Avenue was not the original entrance. That was built later in 1921 when The Plaza extension on the 58th Street side of the hotel was built. Originally they had restaurants on Fifth Avenue: The Rose Room restaurant, the champagne porch and the ladies restaurant. All were in that area."

So, if you were arriving at the hotel on that first day, you would have pulled up at the main entrance on 59th Street in — well, the mode of conveyance was also an interesting part of Opening Day at The Plaza.

That was very nearly the first day you had your choice of arriving at a hotel in your horse-drawn carriage or in one of the motorized taxi cabs which had just started. The taxicab company, in fact, was hoping some of the lavish publicity accompanying the hotel opening would rub off on the spanking new fleet. When the hotel's doors did open up, a running battle ensued outside — shouts and insults mostly — between the taxicab drivers and those perched high on the handsoms. Meanwhile, the owner of the taxis sat safely in the Men's Dining Room, observing the combatants outside.

Harry Allen began his Plaza based motorized taxi service with a fleet of some two dozen green "auto cars" with red stripes the very day The Plaza opened. By the following year his fleet had grown to 600, vastly outnumbering the competing horse drawn carriages which over the years have dwindled down to several dozen.

Only a year later, The Plaza on November 20, 1908 also pioneered the practice of meeting passenger ships from England, France, and Germany with so-called "seagoing" hotel representatives who would board ships in the harbor before they docked and organize their trip to the hotel. Said manager Sterry: "Hotels have always cared for persons arriving at railroad stations, and the meeting of oceangoing ships in the bay is only a step in advance of the old method."

Not far from Mr. Allen in the Men's Dining Room on that day would be four six-foot high torcheres with frosted globes. A century later, these same torcheres greet guests at the 59th Street entrance of the hotel, together with the two torcheres standing like sentry's on either side of the Fifth Avenue entrance. All of them originally were on the first floor balcony overlooking Fifth Avenue. They were moved to their current positions when the hotel's 300-room addition and new Fifth Avenue entrance were opened in 1921.

We are back in the 21st century, starting on our own modern-day tour of The Plaza, still with our guide Mr. Jacobs, and have just passed those relocated torcheres to enter the main lobby. On the north side, opposite the bank of three wood-paneled elevators, is the Italian marble concierge desk where handsome, dapper concierge Tino Merli holds court beginning at 10:00 A.M. each morning (except Sundays) booking tables at Le Cirque, the Four Seasons and even the more casual neighborhood restaurants just west of The Plaza. He also can recommend tours, museums and even dentists.

Peering down at the gorgeous mosaic floor, our guide begins with, "This floor was the original floor but it was covered up for many years. When they were filming *Home Alone II* they took up the rug so Macaulay Culkin could slide on the floor in a scene from the movie."

The rug never went back. In fact, before the advent of air-conditioning in the 1940s, rugs throughout the hotel were pulled up in the summertime.

"While there's no definitive reason why the double P's graced so many nooks and corners of The Plaza," Jacobs continues, pointing out an ornate pair. "it was the custom of clubs at the turn of the last century to use double letters for logos.

"The PP is evident all over. When Henry Hardenbergh built the hotel he placed the P's all over the hotel except in one area, in the grand ballroom [which wasn't built until 1921]. There's one space over the ballroom which has a PH. Although they built the ballroom in the same style, Hardenbergh did not build the ballroom. So all over they have the P's except over the stage in the ballroom. So this was always a lobby."

Jacobs walks over to the corridor outside the Palm Court. The Palm Court restaurant, which was the original tea room, was always here, whereas the Terrace Room restaurant [west of the Palm Court] was for outside dining. So the original kitchen for the Terrace room and actually for the Oak Room was where the jewelry shops are today. Then when they built the extension on the building, they closed off the Terrace Room [putting in the new grand ballroom] and put stores where the kitchen was for the Terrace and Oak rooms. [Actually, the Oak Room was the Oak Bar which had, indeed, a huge oak bar at one end.] Above the shop areas and entrance of the Oak Room was a library reading room, which is now part of accounting. But that was where guests would go to read newspapers and books."

This activity occurred, of course, in a less harried era, and if you've ever been in a library of a rural resort hotel, such as Mohonk Mountain House in New Paltz, New York, or lodges in the Adirondacks region of New York State, you're familiar with the kind of homey feeling guests may have gotten in The Plaza library. In fact, part of the fascination of this hotel is that its amenities seem to go on forever and this library must have fit right in with this idea.

Just to the left of The Plaza front desk is the safe deposit box room, which replaced the cavernous old Plaza safe, where the Vanderbilts and Wanamakers stored their jewels, and which was removed in the 1950s.

"It was a classic old bank safe you could walk into which once probably temporarily housed more diamond bracelets and rings than any safe outside of David Rockefeller's Chase Manhattan Bank," one Plaza employee recalled for me. And, of course, he doesn't mean just anyone could "walk into" the safe. The Plaza strives to be accommodating, but not that accommodating.

"There was a spiral staircase where the theater desk is now where the guests would go up to the reading room and while away the time," Jacobs resumes. "They didn't have television! The Terrace Room which is in the 'well' of the hotel was open to the elements. It was an outside garden. The Palm Court had a leaded ceiling. It was a leaded glass ceiling with a dome, built like the one in the Ritz Hotel in London. They covered it up for two reasons [in 1944 after Conrad Hilton bought the hotel]. One reason is that they needed a place to put the air-conditioning equipment so they dropped the ceiling. The other reason is that one of the general managers jumped out of his apartment facing the interior of the hotel and crashed through the glass roof — and that was the final straw that made them put in the drop ceiling. There was a dropped ceiling in the corridors as well."

The air-conditioners strike again! First the gorgeous tile floor in the lobby and now the glass ceiling in the Palm Court. So much for modern conveniences. Although one long range Plaza plan calls for removing the current covered ceiling and reinstalling a glass ceiling.

"The Plaza's third manager and its sixth manager both committed suicide and I was its ninth manager so I'm glad in this particular instance that things, which sometime come in threes, didn't," former Plaza general manager Richard Wilhelm once commented to me.

Passing through a short vestibule between One C.P.S. and

the 59th Street lobby, Mr. Jacobs and I pass a large dark painting of The Plaza that looks like, but is not, one of Shinn's works.

"The original Everett Shinns were commissioned for the Oak Bar in the 1930s. Not this one but the murals. This is just a picture which is in the style of Everett Shinn," explains Jacobs, peering at this painting of The Plaza. "The area where the Oak Bar was [now the Oak Room] was E.F. Hutton's office and there was a Fifth Avenue entrance to his office. During the economic downturn of the 1930s, E.F. Hutton left and the room became a storeroom. When E.F Hutton was there, the 'back office' of the brokerage firm was where the Oak Bar, now the Oak Room, is. And the bar was along the back and a lot of people, including George M. Cohan and F. Scott Fitzgerald, would stand up at the bar in the Oak Bar. During Prohibition they took the bar out and they made it into a restaurant. In 1945, what is now called the Oak Bar opened and the three Everett Shinns, one behind the bar and one on each end of the bar, were installed. Actually those paintings are being refurbished now and brought back to their original luster. And they're priceless."

In 1975, The Plaza was purchased by Westin for $25 million. Westin then discovered they had to pay an additional $75,000 for the three Shinns, which had been painted in the 40's. One depicts the Pulitzer Fountain, the second a corner of The Plaza on a snowy night with the George Browne Post-designed Cornelius Vanderbilt II mansion in the background (which, incidentally, was at the time the largest townhouse ever built in America), and, the third, Central Park as it looked on a cold winter night.

The Plaza paintings were among many Shinn did for New York landmarks. Shinn also did eighteen murals that were installed in Broadway's Belasco Theater around the time of the opening of The Plaza in 1907.

On this tour I become keenly aware that one of the added values of staying at The Plaza is treasures such as the Shinn murals. Similar glories surround you at almost every turn. It's almost like staying in Newport's Vanderbilt mansion. I often think this is the closest most of us can get to staying in a palace.

But we have turned our attention now to the shops. "Some of these stores had different uses. One was a famous cigar shop," Jacobs relates. "He used to have cigars floating in water and people would buy their cigars here and take them back to the old Oak Bar to smoke them. Another interesting thing about this area is that right where we have our safe deposit boxes used to be a spiral staircase which went downstairs to a Turkish steam bath and a lot of the city's top people, including Mayor Jimmy Walker, used to take a steam bath downstairs and were served food and drink down there. [Nowadays, the city's mayors get steamed only on television.] There was also a barbershop down there. [There has been a barber shop for many years on the mezzanine level of the Fifth Avenue entrance.] The basement also had two notable restaurants. There was The Grill, which physically was under the Edwardian Room [now One C.P.S., shorthand for the restaurant's theoretical address at the beginning of Central Park South]. Trader Vic's, which specialized in Americanized Polynesian food, was under where the current Oak Room restaurant and the Oak Bar are today."

The Grill Room, a favorite of F. Scott Fitzgerald, and even Rudolph Valentino and Gloria Swanson, closed soon after the stock market crash in 1929. Physically, it was almost directly below what was once the Men's Grill, which became the Edwardian Room and is now One C.P.S.. Fitzgerald, who frequented the Grill Room even when he didn't have the money to stay at The Plaza, paid $7 a bottle for gin stored in a subbasement wine cellar of The Plaza.

It's strange Fitzgerald and his bride, the former Zelda Sayre, didn't spend their honeymoon at The Plaza, a place he practically worshiped. In *The Great Gatsby*, for just one example, a character is seen "sitting up very straight on a straight chair in the tea garden of The Plaza." Rather, on April 3, 1920, a week after his first book *This Side of Paradise* was published, the newlyweds checked into suite 2109 of The Biltmore Hotel on East 43rd Street between Madison and Vanderbilt Avenues. Fitzgerald did stay at The Plaza occasionally, and when the couple moved to 38 West 59th Street in October 1920, where they would remain until the following spring, they frequently ordered "room service" from The Plaza because neither was much of a homemaker. World-class frolicker that he was, Fitzgerald did have a propensity for getting tossed out of other New York hotels, so it's possible he simply had too much respect for the place to stay there during his wilder flings.

The glamorous Persian Room was the natural successor to the Grill Room, the scene of "the Years of of the Great Tea Dance," as Fitzgerald described it. Here in the early years of Prohibition, Lucius Beebe would later recall, "when the toddle was in vogue and the academic existence of a generation known as 'collegiate' was orchestrated to the tune of 'Valencia' and 'Kalua Bay,' the fashionable youths of Harvard, Yale and Princeton were accustomed to foregather, especially on Friday and Saturday afternoons, fortified with Matt Winkle's or Dan Moriarity's gin and heartened by the presence of Miss Constance Bennett and other notable prom-trotters of the Stutz Bearcat age."

Moving us along to the English-themed Oak Room, our guide explains, "Everything is original in this room except the tapestries, which were brought in by Mrs. Trump. She did it to soften this room up. The room was built as a bar, so everything in this room has a German drinking theme. The paintings of the three castles are renditions of three famous German castles.

"The coats of arms are from German families. On the chandelier you have a beer drinker with the PP emblem across him and a beer stein in his hand. The original Oak Bar had a water fountain in the middle of the room."

We move to what is now called the Oak Bar, which at the

time of my tour in March 2001 was undergoing renovation and was closed for business. The oak-planked floor was being sanded and there was sawdust everywhere. "There's a new floor in here," Jacobs says, then says hello to the workmen.

"We're putting a few more coats on the floor and then we're done," one of the workmen offers. The three Shinn works, being renovated, are nowhere to be seen.

"My understanding is that they finished the wall because the Everett Shinn paintings weren't ready," Jacobs explains. "We're putting in a new air-conditioning system and a new floor. But when he took the floor up to put in a new floor we found original tiles. But we decided the wood floor more fits the style of the room."

Turning toward Fifth Avenue, we pass The Plaza's newest restaurant, One C.P.S., designed by Adam Tihany. While Tihany bleached the dark walls wood-paneled walls of the Edwardian Room white and covered the huge chandeliers with red lamp shades, he left much of the Edwardian Room intact, including its old world decorative beamed ceiling.

Playwright Neil Simon thanked The Plaza for the multimillion dollar success of *Plaza Suite* by hosting the opening night party for the comedy in the Edwardian Room. Several years later toward the end of the 1960's when his *The Prisoner of Second Avenue* opened on Broadway, about some of the problems associated with living in New York City, Simon also choose the Edwardian Room for the party but by then it had been transformed into The Green Tulip restaurant after much criticism. The Green Tulip soon closed and the Edwardian Room mercifully reopened.

"It has a new refreshing look," Jacobs opines of One C.P.S. As we proceed further along toward what is now the Fifth Avenue entrance, he continues: "There was no entrance on Fifth Avenue originally. The Rose Room [which is used for private functions] originally was a restaurant called the Rose Restaurant. This area here," he points out, referring to a location immediately inside what is now the Fifth Avenue entrance to the hotel, "and the area where the front of the hotel is was the area called the champagne porch, which was open only in the summertime."

If you have ever been to Atlanta's Georgian Terrace Hotel and dined on its terrace you might understand some of the feeling of dining at The Plaza's Terrace restaurant. Unlike the Georgian Terrace, The Plaza has the added advantage of being on Central Park.

"When the Rose Room closed," Jacobs resumes, "it became the Persian Room. And then the Persian Room closed and it was a Studebaker dealer for a while and then a dress shop.

We move outside as the traffic from Fifth Avenue whizzes by. Right in front of the Fifth Avenue entrance to The Plaza is the only street in New York with no name. "It's just the drive-way to The Plaza. It has no name. Public street but no name," Jacobs says. Moving a little to the right of the Fifth Avenue entrance of The Plaza we come upon some huge stone stairs peppered with stubby stone spikes and blocked by flower boxes. "These were the steps and that was the entrance way to the champagne porch," Jacobs elucidates.

Going back inside the "new" Fifth Avenue entrance, built when the 1921 addition was added, Jacobs points to the balcony level which I remembered as the location of a barbershop when I was a little boy. There's still a barbershop there but also a business center. "Where the barbershop is was also part of the champagne porch," Jacobs further enlightens us.

The Palm Court, originally called the "tea court," was furnished with green and white tables in the style of the Petite Trianon. It's bestowed with large potted palms and hedged in by flowering azaleas. Its caryatids are copies of originals made by Donato Donato, a student of Michelangelo. The Palm Court's marble pillars and oversized pedestal hurricane lamps also add credibility to claims The Plaza in one sense is really the most magnificent French chateau in the world.

As we skirt the Palm Court, a violinist and pianist are playing songs from the score of the Broadway musical *The King and*

I, including "Shall We Dance?" If you happened by The Palm Court in 1952, the year Gertrude Lawrence, who co-starred in *The King and I* with Yul Brenner, died you would have also heard selections from the famed Rodgers and Hammerstein musical being played in loving memory of the star who was staying at The Plaza when her autobiography was published. She entertained lavishly in her suite, sometimes dispatching William Hood, her loyal chauffeur for many years, to fetch guests who hated to negotiate with New York City cabs and cabbies. Loving to cook, she was spotted in The Plaza kitchen helping the chef prepare for her guests. When she died of cancer, some of The Plaza staff, who she tipped generously and always had a kind word for, took it hard. At her death, her life-long friend Noël Coward, who co-starred with her in a number of his own theatrical creations both on Broadway and in London's West End, cabled, "I shall miss her as long as I live." Ed Sullivan said Lawrence was "a shimmering, glittering ornament on the theater's Christmas tree."

Pushing back the huge mirrored doors at the rear of the Palm Court and ascending a wide marble staircase we come upon five crystal chandeliers with ties to both Versailles and Czarist Russia. They are the copies, mentioned above, made by Charles Winston, the brother of jeweler Harry Winston and commissioned by that flamboyant Russian immigrant Serge Obolensky.

Walking left around the Palm Court toward the 58th Street side of the hotel and past the 58th Street side of the elevator bank but not getting to the gift shop yet, Jacobs pauses. "The original hotel stopped right here where this staircase is. You can see it from outside by the way the color of the brick changes. The original ballroom was in the Baroque Room (on the second floor overlooking Central Park). When they took out the stage of the original ballroom they built the general manager's office [on the second floor] above it. The hydraulic stage is long gone."

Moving westward, we arrive at the entrance to the Oyster

Bar restaurant. "The Oyster Bar opened in 1969. First it was a pharmacy. Then it became the employee's cafeteria. Then it became part of the loading dock of the hotel and then the Oyster Bar."

A security guard lets us pass through a nondescript door leading downstairs. "We'll go down to the kitchen and I'll give you to Executive Chef Bruno Tison," Jacobs says. "He can give you to Bill O'Brien who can show you the lower level. Now, all this area back here is where Trader Vic's used to be."

It is here that 70-year-old Eugene Lapersuque, The Plaza's very first executive chef (and who had been the chef for the Rothchilds banking family, as well as Delmonico's in New York), first reigned in 1907, with menus that included wild grouse and partridge as well as the more commonplace duck and lobster. The kitchen's first real test came when Fred Sterry hosted a luncheon for a hundred VIPs, including some permanent guests and journalists, on September 30, 1907, the day before the hotel officially opened. But even the Filets de Boeuf à l'Arlequin and Glace Napolitaine paled compared to the seemingly endless gilded rooms of carved marble and wood that these first guests saw that day.

Jacobs and I part company. Before we do he can't help but add, "This is a very old world kitchen. Years ago all of the food used to come out of one line. The one line in front of his [Bruno's, or the head chef's] office. You had one chef who used to call out all the orders for seven restaurants. They would put the orders on trays whether prime ribs or lobster and take it to the different restaurants. They were always walking up and down stairs. Now the Oyster Bar has its own kitchen. One C.P.S. has its own kitchen. At one time all the food came to the central kitchen and to the executive chef. The most famous one recently was Trombetti. He was here for nearly thirty years."

Bruno Tison's small 10-by-15-square-foot office is the calm at the center of the storm of The Plaza's cavernous kitchen. It's oh so quiet compared to the cacophony outside. Silverware clanking. Dishes being stacked and readied to receive food. Tison has movie star good looks, even a touch of Marlon Brando about him.

"Many things have changed," he ably, almost seamlessly, takes over where Jacobs left off. "For example, in 1959, the only spoken language in this kitchen was French. It's only since the 1960s that it's slowly started to change. Now we have to learn Spanish!" Tison laughs. "Between chefs and sous-chefs we have about 90 people in the kitchen on the average. Some peak times we have 100 or 105. We've gone as high as 135 when we had Trader Vic's and the Edwardian Room was still working under us. This where we are is the main kitchen."

We spot a chef who's cooking roasts. "He's prepping for a banquet. This is going to be the sauce. There's a little tasting going on. This is the kitchen dining room where we do the tasting for private banquets."

Next we stroll into the small but nonetheless most exclusive dining room. About as big as an officers mess on shipboard, with a plain wooden table that can comfortably seat eight, this is where Mick Jagger had his 50th birthday party in 1993 in privacy far removed from the prying lenses of tabloid photographers. Jagger had had well publicized affairs, everyone from Brigitte Bardot to Brazilian model Lucina Morad, who broke up his thirteen-year relationship to model Jerry Hall in 1999. But his private bash was so secret that some of the waitresses who served the rock superstar didn't know who they were working for until they came into the small approximately 12-foot-by-8-foot room. "It's always been here," explains Tison of the space.

In recent years, Chef Tison was flown by the King of Morocco, a frequent Plaza guest, to his palace to train the king's staff how to select, season, prepare and present meat dishes. In 1998, he received rave reviews for preparing the dinner for 1,400 people at *Time* magazine's 70th anniversary where Julia Child received the "Silver Spoon" award of the decade. Tison himself was awarded the "Silver Spoon" in November 1999.

For the 75th anniversary of *Time*, Tison recalls "we built a kitchen in a tent on the north side [50th street] side of Radio City Music Hall. And we created a few tiny satellite kitchens and we served the canapés from the satellite kitchens. Each chef from each satellite kitchen came and we finished the plate on the table. The main course was something that I baked at The Plaza and I put everything into food warmers into a food truck and drove downtown to Radio City. And for deserts we ordered the deserts from The Plaza Hotel. They were 50 percent finished and we put the deserts down on the table and finished them on the table."

"Bruno's a stickler for detail and possesses incredible focus and pride in his work," Mark Huntley, general manager of The Fairmont Hotel in San Francisco, told *Food Arts* magazine. Huntley, it seems, also persuaded the renowned chef to stay on as chef of the Palm Court of The Plaza where he was soon after promoted to executive chef of the entire hotel.

We continue to move past vats and stacks of stainless steel pots. "All the vegetables are done here, the soups, the banquets and the employee cafeteria. We feed about 1,000 people a day in the employee cafeteria. And in the restaurants we feed about an average of 3,000 people a day, 3,000 customers. We have 1000 to 1250 employees, depending on the season. They eat very well. They're the most difficult customers to please but they get good food. I eat it every day. Then we have the butchers. We have two butchers. The meat butcher. The fish butcher."

We walk into cavernous freezer lockers piled high with steaks, then move on to another series of stainless tables. "This is an area where we do a lot of cold prep work and salads. Over here is a produce box which connects to a huge storeroom." It's piled high with carrots and vegetables and there's plenty of fresh running water flowing over the stainless steel counters and the tile floors. Tison pauses to talk shop, and chop, with one chef: "The venison is for next week. The antelope leg is for this Sunday brunch."

"This is the pastry shop," Tison says as we arrive at it. "The Plaza doesn't bring any pastries in from other locations; everything originates here. Everything is homemade as you can see." He tries one of the cookies. "Are you chief taster?" I ask. "Yes, right!" he laughs. Eric, the pastry chef, shows us what seem to be dozens of chocolate cups filled with cappuccino. And that's exactly what they are. They are solid chocolate, filed with cappuccino and liquor. "We have fresh croissants, brioche, coffee cake. Even simple cookies — everything is made here," Tison proudly states. "This guy is making the scones for tea time. It's a massive, massive production house. You know, a lot of times, large hotels are associated with poor quality food. But you can see what we use here. Only the best and freshest of food and produce. The best strawberries, the best . . . " he trails off, allowing us simply to imagine the enormous length a complete explication of such dedicated expertise would reach.

"This banquet, they ordered a combination plate of deserts. So we make them very, very small, miniature sized. This is our pie room; it's all air-conditioned and kept very cold. This is where all the doughs are made and the baker works here at night. He does all his croissants, muffins, Danish. Eleven at night he comes in and at 6:00 A.M. in the morning everything is fresh. This is our ice cream room. This guy judges all the ice creams. We make all of our own ice creams except we have a little promotion deal with Haagen-Daz. We use Haagen-Daz ice cream in all our restaurants but for our banquets we do everything ourselves. I still think our ice cream, although Hagen-Daz [he hastens to add] has an excellent product, we make it even better. First of all it's much more economical to make your own ice cream yourself. Second of all, in banquets, you have so many flavors that Hagen-Daz doesn't carry. We even cream new ice creams for banquets with different sherbets. People suggest flavors sometimes that are not even in the book!"

Tison beams with pride while taking me next on a tour of

the Oyster Bar kitchen located on the same floor as the Oyster Bar itself. "The oyster shucker that works here. He told me, 'Oh chef, chef, I've never done that!' But he learned it very fast. In a couple of days they get it. The Oyster Bar is very, very popular. I think the reason it's very popular is that the atmosphere is very casual." Indeed, it has the relaxing atmosphere of an English pub. "It's informal; it's also the only place in the hotel that you can smoke a cigar and eat other than the Oak Room. Our menu is very, very simple. It's kind of American continental food with a touch of French and South American dishes. Because we do have a very strong South American clientele here."

While the restaurant has only 71 seats in peak months like December it does some 800 "covers," or the combined number of lunches and dinners. "Every seat turns over very fast. Some in 50 minutes." And no request is turned down by the Oyster Bar or any of the other restaurant as long as guests give the hotel enough time to prepare something.

"As long as it is on the market I will get it — unless there is a snowstorm!" proclaims Tison. The Plaza staff in general will try to meet any, let us say, reasonable request. On the more romantic side, the service staff once threw rose pedals over a bed for a couple that was having their anniversary at The Plaza.

We pass several huge vats where spaghetti will be cooked later for room service orders and where back in the 1940's, Paul Boiardi, a maitre d' hotel, cooked his own recipe of spaghetti for Mr. and Mrs. John Hartford of the A & P supermarket family (whose first food store was on Manhattan's Vesey Street). It was then that the ebullient Boiardi confided to Mr. Hartford that his dream was mass producing his spaghetti and some years later the Chef Boyardee brand became a household name.

It took Tison some time before he himself could find his way around the back of the house. "I can't say I mastered everything but in a week or ten days you get a feeling of where you . . . " He trails off again, as we trail doggedly after him.

From the Oyster Bar kitchen, we snake around to the Palm Court kitchen. "We do the hot food downstairs and the cold, salads and such upstairs right in back of the Palm Court."

We are about to voyage even further downstairs in the good ship Plaza. But first we must wait for our next expert guide — William O'Brien, assistant food and beverage director. He promptly arrives, Tison bids us adieu, and, reveries of the Pastry Room still not entirely driven from our mind, we push on.

During peak occupancy, room service receives some 500-600 orders for breakfast, O'Brien commences, as competently as his predecessors. "You order at 7:00, we deliver fifteen minutes from the time you ordered," he explains, as though, like some famished account exec from Dubuque up in suite 1041 we might shoot back with a complaint for even this scant degree of tardiness.

Between room service and the hotel's five dining rooms (including the Oak Bar for light meals), several thousand meals are served each day at The Plaza. And this number can easily double when there are big banquets and weddings in the Grand Ballroom.

"In the evening it usually takes 30 to 45 minutes being that it takes a little bit longer to cook some meals like steak," O'Brien continues. "But breakfast we usually try and do it between 20 and 30 minutes. We also have the butler program. So if you are a VIP the butlers check with us how fast we can process an order and they'll come down and expedite an order. So if we're really busy they'll come down and expedite an order, especially in September when you have ten or fifteen delegations. If you want to take a picnic basket to Central Park you call down to room service and order your picnic basket and have it delivered to your room and you go out to lunch. Those are the fun things. We'll do different types of lunches. We'll change it June, July and August. There will be a special card in the room. Salads. A bottle of wine. We try and keep it really simple."

We voyage ever downward to the subbasement. "Where are we now?" I inquire. "You're in the subbasement," he answers. "We came from the kitchen area and now you're in the subbasement. The subbasement is the laundry area. I'll take you down to where I believe the old coal room was."

My biggest impression of the subbasement, and of the floor below the subbasement, is how huge this area is. It seems the levels are several stories high each. We proceed down a long flight of stairs into the bowels of the ship Plaza. In fact, I get the distinct feeling of what it must be like to be in the engine room of a vast ocean liner. There's the sound of the rush of steam. Huge washing and drying machines whirling. When we reach the third subbasement, Bill says, "This is it. This is what is left of the coal room. We're at 59th Street at the northwest corner of the hotel." Bill points to the ceiling directly above us, "The old Trader Vic's restaurant. It was right in that area there. We're down below that. The old Trader Vic's used to be right in this area here one flight up. I've never walked the tracks but there they are."

The mention of Trader Vic's brings to my mind the time Plaza owner Paul Sonnabend was asked if he felt the new Trader Vic's restaurant would be cost effective given its $1 million price tag. He said, "The only way I can answer that question is to remind you that the space now occupied by Trader Vic's was previously a barber shop that paid me $14,000 a year. We estimate that Trader Vic's will gross $2.3 million a year." He was right. It was a very good trade.

O'Brien, meanwhile, further explains, "The tunnel to ferry coal into the hotel to operate its enormous boilers was at the opposite end of the hotel on the Central Park South side of the hotel below where Trader Vic's was and where the Spa is now. The train tracks were actually down in the northwest corner of the hotel and came from a siding in which they brought the coal cars in, similar to the situation on a much smaller scale that The Waldorf-Astoria had. They used to bring VIPs in on private rail cars under that hotel; this was on a much smaller scale."

We see sections of dirt-coated stainless steel tracks and we walk along them heading from what must be Central Park South to the 58th Street side of the hotel. "There's an elevator now that goes up and down to the street level. So right here, when we're here, you can feel the coldness. The tracks would come all the way over here. There are the imprints," he points out.

"There were two sets of railroad tracks up and down Manhattan. The tracks on Park Avenue were used mostly for passenger trains and those on the West Side were for freight predominantly," explains former Plaza manager Richard Wilhelm, who has studied the hotel's history. "And the tracks on the West Side actually had a spur that went under 59th Street and coal came into a below-ground entrance on the Northwest corner. The Plaza was really a very large hotel and there was tremendous demand for coal because all the heating and hot water was generated with coal. And coal burns very fast. So there was a lot of demand for coal and it came into the hotel on small railroad cars underground so it wouldn't disrupt any of the activity of the hotel."

These Plaza tracks were also part of a larger extensive underground network of tunnels and tracks used to ferry coal and supplies to hotels on Fifth Avenue which were wholly apart from the larger maze of subway tunnels and manholes leading to viaducts for sewers and electric lines of subterranean Manhattan. After The Savoy-Plaza was built in 1927, a tunnel from The Plaza to the Savoy-Plaza across Fifth Avenue was used to take food that had been initially prepared or "prepped" in the cavernous Plaza kitchen to The Savoy-Plaza to be "finished" and/or reheated.

During Prohibition, this same tunnel was allegedly used to ferry illicit liquor, which was stored in the subbasement of The Plaza, to other hotels and drop-off points.

The small section of stainless steel actually stops near 59th

Street and there are left only the imprints or vague outlines of where the tracks once were. Nearby, where the old wine cellar used to be, the walls are being renovated. It's not that this sub-basement area would ever be used for offices, let alone rooms, but its ongoing renovation is indicative of the immense job it is to keep the back of the house ship shape.

"The original door of the wine cellar is still there. You can still see it," O'Brien says. "We actually moved the wine cellar to another location. But we use a couple of the original vaults for some of our champagne." Today, The Plaza's extensive wine cellar is on the kitchen level of the hotel and is complete with thousands of bottles of Mumms and Bollinger and Veuve Clicquot.

Like everywhere else The Plaza by law was forbidden to sell liquor during Prohibition. "But it had a cache of champagne and liquor stored in the basement for discreet clientele who lived in the hotel," confesses Wilhelm. "Some was carried through a tunnel which ran underneath Fifth Avenue from The Plaza to The Savoy-Plaza. They ferried a lot of stuff back and forth and somewhere down in the third subbasement there's still the outline of where the tunnel was bricked up on The Plaza side. Over the years parts of the tunnel were demolished. But during Prohibition they actually used that tunnel to cart liquor back and forth and in fact, used it to store liquor." Wilhelm once made a more pleasant discovery in his own second-floor manager's office: one of The Plaza's original architects had used it many decades earlier.

Moving toward Fifth Avenue, the whirl of the massive clothes dryers becomes almost deafening.

From the third subbasement we go up to The Plaza heavens. Up to the 17th floor, where there are no guest rooms except the first floor of The Plaza's penthouse. "All these are either storage rooms or we have a couple of offices here also. The butler has his office here and he shares the office with someone else," explains yet another guide. We open a room which is on the Fifth Avenue side of the building. It has a two-story gabled ceiling and a great view of Fifth Avenue. It's number 1735. We come upon a huge interior suite right out of *Jane Eyre*, which is filled with furniture waiting to be reupholstered and finished.

"Years ago a number of the small rooms on the Park, Fifth Avenue and 58th Street were occupied by staff of the wealthy families which had suites downstairs."

The 1940s ushered in the lavishly appointed office of *Gourmet* magazine which leased the 22-room penthouse for its world headquarters. The space was originally the residence of Canadian Harry S. Black, whose construction firm built The Plaza. The *Gourmet* offices included a 60-foot drawing room, marble foyer and solid gold-bathroom fixtures in one of the lavatories.

Walking south on the 17th Floor to the 58th Street side of the hotel and walking as far as we can go to the west we come upon the door which leads to the penthouse proper. The Plaza Presidential Suite (which is also known as the Penthouse Suite), at 7,802 square feet, is basically a townhouse in the sky, with an immense terrace and triple-story living room with magnificent view of Central Park through enormous nearly floor-to-ceiling windows. A sauna comes with the $15,000 a night price-tag

Like the calm before the Dot.com and high-tech stock slide of 2001, savvy pre-1929 crash investors knew they were literally living on borrowed money. Black became so depressed by what he felt would mushroom into a huge downward spiral he actually tried to commit suicide in his 17th floor penthouse suite by drowning himself in his bathtub. His flustered butler thought his employer had fallen asleep rather than purposefully attempting to end his life. But a half year later, the 66-year old Canadian developer, then reeling from the full gale force of the market crash, shot himself to death at his Lloyds Harbor, Long Island, estate. Black's partner, Bernhard Beinecke died of natural causes two years later in his Plaza suite.

After passing a series of smaller rooms which are some-times used as bedrooms for staffers of those who rent the pent-house suite today (these are furnished as actual hotel rooms, as opposed to those other staff rooms noted above which can also be storage, changing or utility rooms), you enter a large fabric-lined round foyer with a steep stairway leading to the 18th floor and the heart of the penthouse — a cavernous room with triple height windows overlooking Central Park (even though perched on the non-park 58th Street side of the hotel). By contrast, its 18th floor bedrooms are modest, about the size of the average big park-view rooms in the hotel. The other fab-ulous feature of the penthouse is a large terrace for outdoor parties. Its fully equipped kitchen — including such indis-pensables as a washer and dryer and wine cellar — may pale next to Martha Stewart's fabulous series of stoves, fridges and sinks on her TV show but is more than adequate for the head of state who brings his own chef and staff.

Today, The Plaza has a total of sixty suites among its approximately 805 "keys" to suites and single rooms, accord-ing to John Maibach, director of the hotel's room division. These range from the cavernous Presidential Suite, 1801 (with its five bedrooms and terrace overlooking the park) and where in April 2001 Woody Allen was shooting a movie, to four other so-called "specialty suites." There are also twenty Plaza Suites, corner apartments on the northeast and southeast corners of the hotel all overlooking Fifth Avenue (with only those on the Northeast corner having views of Central Park). It was in a Plaza suite in which Neil Simon set, perhaps it goes without saying, his play of the same name.

"The Plaza suites are on floors two to fourteen and not on every floor," Maibach explains. Besides the Vanderbilt Suite (a favorite place to stay of Plaza co-owners Chairman Kwek and Prince Alwaleed), the other four specialty suites include the Presidential Suite, Astor Suite, and the Louis XIV Suite on the tenth floor of the hotel. The Astor Suite was where Michael Douglas and Catherine Zeta-Jones spent their honeymoon night in November 2000 after they were married in the hotel's grand ballroom. The fifth floor Vanderbilt Suite, with its gargantuan living room the size of three large bedrooms, can expand to a suite with five bedrooms.

Suites and rooms at The Plaza have always being redecorated to comply with the tastes and desires of various owners and managers over the years but seldom have so many rooms been repainted almost simultaneously as there were in 1959 when John G. Horsman was the hotel's general manager (at a time when Hilton still owned The Plaza). Horsman saw to it that some 342 of the hotel's roughly 1000 rooms were completely repainted, while at the same time renovating three of its deluxe suites, including one that had been occupied for a half century by a Miss Susan Duncan, and which had been decorated personally by Elsie de Wolfe Mendle (Lady Mendle), America's first women decorator.

It's also interesting to note that a number of the second floor function rooms that face Central Park and Fifth Avenue were once upon a time actually the hotel's choicest guest suites, with their elaborated-carved marble fireplaces, mirrored doors and ornate chandeliers.

A while later I head back to my somewhat more modest room on the 58th street side of the hotel to relax and order some coffee. After visiting the ghosts of the past in the basement and subbasements I spy a curious almost ghostly sight from the window of my room facing the 58th Street side of The Plaza and Bergdorf-Goodman and what was been known as the Avon Building with its enormous glass face. In that glass face I could make out with photographic precision the exterior of The Plaza's Penthouse Suite, literally perched on the topmost portion of the hotel's southwest corner.

"I've been in this place like seventeen, it's going to be eighteen years and it has been fabulous to work here. It's the best place to work. I've seen a lot of celebrities here," Angel Betamces, my room service waiter later informs me.

"I served Michael Douglas and I met his wife, Catherine

Zeta-Jones. When they spent like two days here before the wedding. Doing the preparation. They were bringing all the flowers. They were in the Astor Suite. I didn't have too much time to talk to her. Very nice. I met John Boy, I met Sugar Ray Leonard, Mohammed Ali. You name it, I met a lot of people here. Anthony Perkins. In fact, yesterday, the Indiana Pacers were staying here. . . . [Over the years, a number of professional teams, among them The Miami Heat and Chicago Bulls stayed at The Plaza while in town to play the New York Knicks.] The Astor Suite's got the view, the view of the park. It's got the Jacuzzi, the faucets in gold."

※

I get a chance to begin work in room service the following morning. I get there at 7:00 A.M., and tables are lined up like planes ready to take off. "Overnight we collect the room service orders from the doorknobs and we take them out forty minutes in advance and we send the order to get it ready," recounts Karim El-Rami, Director of Private Dining at The Plaza. "So, let's say 7:15 delivery. That would go up at 6:55 A.M. [on the board]. It takes five to ten minutes to prepare."

Orders come into a central room and the room service manager on duty organizes the tables according to time much the same as a flight controller does at the airport. The written orders are called into the room of service chefs who prepare the eggs just as the tables are pushed in front of their large hotel griddles. "When the cashier gets them she gives them to me and I tell the waiters if there's no special event. They've been here for years so they know right what to do. If there's a specific thing on the order that's unusual I make sure it's on the tray. Every waiter has a table ready to go. They get the coffee fresh and fresh milk and then if there's food they go down here around the bend to the chef. If they get the food first and go back and get the coffee if would be a waste of time . . . If they order a steak it takes longer. The order taken tells the guest exactly how much time it takes."

As we talk the order taker's voice comes over the loud-speaker loud and clear: "we have a guest that needs coffee right away . . . "

"I would say that *before* 6:00 A.M. we get someone who wants to eat a little something unusual. They want a fresh fish. People who travel from oversees there's a big time difference and morning is sometimes lunch or dinner for them. Like now in Egypt it's like 2:00 P.M. in the afternoon. When someone orders a beer at 10:00 in the morning you know they're used to having a beer at happy hour in England. Whatever they want at anytime we will get it for them. We have that kind of attitude. We get a lot of people who say they want it 'now!' It happens. They say, 'If you can't bring it up in five minutes don't bring it up.' Some people put their orders on the door-knob cards and forget to put the room number on it. Those that pick them up at 2:00 A.M., you have to tell them to check the room numbers even before they take it off the doorknobs but sometimes they don't."

Now there's a hotel tip for every paying guest. Remember to write down your room number. The Plaza staff will strive, as this tour has just extravagantly shown, to do whatever it can for you, but even they can't read your mind.

Conrad, Zsa Zsa, Donald, and Ivana

World War II was raging overseas when The Plaza faced its own first serious invasion. The assault arrived in the guise of a tall half-patrician, half-good-ole-boy, churchgoing workaholic whose name and nature would soon change the very course of world hotel history. Conrad Hilton sent shivers of revolt and revulsion through the hearts of many Plazaphiles on both sides of the front desk. They envisioned an end of the era where the customer was always right and the beginning of a relentless towing to a bottomless bottom-line. And blame it all on one Zsa Zsa Gabor.

Conrad Hilton's 1941 chance meeting with Hungarian sex siren Zsa Zsa Gabor at a party set the stage for his purchase of The Plaza two years later in October 1943.

Hilton in his autobiography *Be My Guest* recalls, "I met the foreign charmer at a party. She was blonde, witty, vivacious, and just off the boat. This fascinating package, Zsa Zsa Gabor by name, appealed to me as a most amusing person. Seated next to me at dinner she suddenly did one of those fascinating tricks women do with their eyes and announced: 'theenk I am going to marry you.'

"And I, the confirmed bachelor, to whom marriage from a religious standpoint was a forbidden fruit, [a staunch Roman

Catholic, Hilton had been divorced] thought that was a fine joke. 'Why don't you do that?' I challenged with a roar of laughter.

"The joke was on me."

Hilton married Zsa Zsa in April 1943.

"Our marriage was doomed before it started. I could afford it, yes. Glamour, I found, is expensive, and Zsa Zsa was glamour raised to the last degree. She also knew more days on which gifts could be given than appear on any holiday calendar. And then, of course, you could always give gifts because it was no special day at all and thereby transform it.

"But Zsa Zsa was not always on the receiving end by any manner of means."

To Hilton, Zsa Zsa not only added the woman's touch, but a glamour that, as a hard-nosed businessman accustomed to dealing mostly with men, was virtually unknown to him at this time.

In the spring of 1943, Hilton, who had his heart set on The Waldorf-Astoria, bought the Roosevelt, and with Zsa Zsa at his side spent more and more time in New York, the city of his biggest business dreams. The Plaza was next.

"After thirty-six years under one continuous original management, the hotel was passing into other hands," writes Eve Brown. "The world-acclaimed hostelry which cost twelve million dollars to build in 1907 and which could not be duplicated for forty million dollars in the twenties or recreated at any price during World War II, went, at the height of that war, to Conrad Hilton for $7,400,000.

"Consternation swept through the corridors. For Plaza tenants the name Hilton Hotel meant only one thing — a commercial hotel. Little old ladies with large pocketbooks whispered, 'It can't happen here,' and as it turned out, it didn't. Even Hilton, the bold boniface, was cognizant of the very special aura which surrounded The Plaza, and was determined to keep it so. But he had to win his battle for popularity and the admiration of his tenants."

Buying the hotel was the easy part. "By 1943, the situation was so critical that The Plaza had to be put up for sale," Brown continues. "Edwin Beinecke was then serving as deputy commissioner of the American Red Cross in London, and he and his brother Frederick conferred by transatlantic phone. They wanted to save the fine hotel, wanted it for themselves, for it had been their father's most precious dream fulfilled. The market price of $7,400,000 presented no difficulty, for they had the money, thanks to the conservatism of Ben Beinecke in a boomtime era when everyone else was going speculation mad. But ethics would not permit. Were they, the insiders, to buy the hotel for themselves at that shockingly low price, it might be viewed as less than an arm's length transaction; it might cause those who would lose plenty, the bondholders, to wonder and suspect."

The sale of The Plaza by the United States Realty corporation to Hilton was as much a matter of integrity as Hilton's own business genius. For years, the corporation's bondholders owned all its hotel holdings, including the Savoy Plaza across the street, and had been drawing company reserves. But, instead of trying to postpone the payments, Hilton did what he could to assuage tenants' fears, especially those of "permanents" whose very presence had virtually saved The Plaza from the wrecking ball during the Depression.

"If I had thought the habitués of the Roosevelt were upset by my advent into their midst, The Plaza dwellers, much more bound up in tradition, much more conservative, truly seemed to think my connection with their hotel might mark the end of their world," writes Hilton in his autobiography.

Hilton asked J. B. Herndon to supervise the renovating. "We did not intend to change a thing. Only to refurbish what was there," Hilton further explains. "In the end it cost us almost $6 million.

"The first challenge was to break the ice. We decided to show them we would take nothing away, by restoring a tradition as a gesture of good faith. We gave them back the Oak Bar which had been sacrificed to house a brokerage firm [E.F. Hutton]. The brokerage firm was moved to the mezzanine, the Oak Bar polished to its original luster, and an Oak Room custom of bygone years resurrected. Ladies were not permitted in the Oak Room until after the stock exchange closed. Not only were the gentlemen pleased to recapture an old sanctuary, but the ladies (such is the way of ladies) were delighted to patronize the Oak Room in the late afternoon, feeling as they did that they were invading a masculine world."

"Mr. Hilton came in and out like a prince. Very dignified," remembers Joe Szorentini, who for more than half a century was a doorman at The Plaza. "He would nod and talk to practically everybody even though he owned the place. He was real polite and very humble. He was very religious."

Does Joe remember Zsa Zsa?

Yes he does: "I remember seeing Zsa Zsa a few times. Her mother used to run a jewelry shop on Madison Avenue and Zsa Zsa went there quite often."

A Hungarian refugee, Zsa Zsa, whose original named was Sari, escaped from Nazi persecution of Eastern Europe to become Conrad Hilton's queen of The Plaza decades before Ivana Trump. But as flamboyant and unpredictable as she herself was she was taken completely by surprise by the antics of husband Conrad who got up at a Travelers Aid Society benefit at The Persian Room one night and proceeded to make a bit of a spectacle of himself doing the Varsoviana, which was a dance from his native New Mexico. Nothing would have been made of it other than giggles from the guests in the room had not one society columnist of the day chosen to "review" Mr. Hilton's dancing, calling it awkward and slightly embarrassing.

Joe's wife, Veronica, remembers meeting Conrad Hilton while she waited for Joe in the lobby. She was awestruck but Hilton said, "Don't be in awe of me. I'm just like everyone else."

"He was the nicest person, but the only owner I ever met. He said, 'Any time you want to stay in any one of our hotels, just get in touch with them and tell them you know me, and I'll put you up wherever you want to go.'"

In the early 1950s, the height of the Hilton reign, glamour was the order of the decade. According to one Plaza memo dated January 2, 1952:

"In a setting simulating the court of King Louis XVI, the seventh annual Yuletide Assembly was held last night (Friday) in the Grand Ballroom of The Plaza to benefit the Youth Consultation Service of the Episcopal Diocese of New York. Lester Lanin and his orchestra furnished the music for the ball and also played for dancing in the Terrace Room, where numerous dinners were given for debutantes making their formal debuts in society.

"Red, blue and silver formed the decorative motif for the fete. On the stage in the ballroom, where a pageant represented a reception held by the King of France and Marie Antoinette, tapestries from French and Company pictured events of court life. Tall urns at each side of the stage held pink quince, dogwood and silvered sprays of meilox. The ballroom boxes were decorated with the same blossoms and with blue and silver ribbons.

"Miss Diana Tailer, debutante daughter of Mrs. Stanley Martineau and Mr. T. Suffern Tailer, as Queen Marie Antoinette, and Mr. Courtney Ford Ellis, as the king, sat on throne chairs during the pageant. Members of the court surrounding them included Miss Audrey Waqstaff as the French Princess Royal; Miss Cordelia Eleanor Lowry as Madame Elizabeth; Miss Vera Lawrence Whitmore as the Dutchesse de Polignae, and the Misses Anne Laler and Margot Potter as Dames d'Honour.

"The guests at court were entertained by a gavotte danced by the king's brother Artoir, represented by Mr. Frank Osgood Butler, 2nd, with Miss Daphne Suthers."

❈

International hostess and interior designer Elsie de Wolfe [Lady Mendle] was brought in by Plaza promotion director Serge

Obolensky in 1944 to design a special suite and, more importantly, to show that The Plaza had lost none of its fashionability since Conrad Hilton added it to his growing chain of hotel properties.

As Obolensky saw it, the suite would be called the Lady Mendle suite, which today would be tantamount to calling something the Martha Stewart suite. De Wolfe lived mostly in Europe at the time, and came to New York once a year for an extended period of time. Obolensky thought, and rightly so, that her touch would be an excellent publicity gimmick as well as a welcome homage to her high style.

"It was a lavish apartment decorated in the same shades of green and white she had used at The St. Regis and The Beverly Hills," writes Jane Smith in her biography, *Elsie de Wolfe: A Life in High Style.*

"The draperies and covers for the chair were in the fern-painted chintz she had discovered for her own house in Beverly Hills, and one of the more prominent pieces of furniture was a white-painted secretary with baroque embellishments from Tony Duquette."

Count Vasilli Adlerberg, another displaced Russian aristocrat who was working with Obolensky, recalled, "There was nothing cheap about her. Everything was always the best. She wasn't interested in hearing about the price . . . I will never forget trying to explain to her that white silk wouldn't be practical in a hotel, with the wear and the cleaning. She got very angry. She didn't want to hear about cleaning."

Its lavishness surpassed even the most ornate apartments at the hotel. Cholly Knickerbocker, a New York columnist of the day, and one of Liz Smith's first employers — she used to ghost-write some of his material as was a common practice of the day — called the de Wolfe Plaza suite "Elsie's Folly." No matter to Obolensky. The more press it got — good or bad — the better he liked it. And it had one other added attraction: the designer commandeered it for some of her own lavish parties, making further splashes in the society pages.

Hilton, after buying The Plaza in 1943 during its boom war years for $7.4 million, sold it ten years later to A. M. "Sonny" Sonnabend, head of the Hotel Corporation of America, for $16 million. But as part of the sale of the building, he took an option on the land under the hotel, and sold it at a handsome profit as well.

He also extended his company's management lease until 1960, seven years after he sold the property. Two years before Hilton's lease expired, Sonnabend sold The Plaza in 1958 to financier Lawrence A. Wein for $21 million. Wein gave Sonnabend and his Hotel Corporation of America twenty-five years to run the property.

When Hilton pulled out of the management picture in 1960, the hotel again hit hard times. Room occupancy plunged and the hotel's upkeep soared. The management hired a disciplinarian named Neal Lang, whom hoteliers liken to the Waldorf's Frank Wangeman, who also had worked at The Plaza. Not until Alfonse Salomone, a former Plaza rooms manager, was brought on under this tenure did The Plaza again turn the corner. "In 1964, the occupancy rate had reached 81 percent, five points above New York City's average and twenty points higher than the national average," writes Eve Brown.

The revitalized Plaza had lost one customer, however. Conrad Hilton. When he came to the city now he stayed at The Waldorf-Astoria. The Hilton saga would, strangely, almost replay itself out, complete with femme fatale, several decades later, when another brash "proletarian" real estate mogul came along to do some shopping on fashionable Fifth Avenue.

"Ever since I got out of college, I've had a list of the ten New York properties that I wanted to acquire," Donald Trump writes in his *Trump: Surviving at the Top*. "I'm not ready to reveal what they all are. But, I will say that The Plaza Hotel has always been number one on that list."

In many ways, the story of Donald Trump's rise from the borough of Queens, as the son of a builder who manufactured middle-income apartment housing, to become the man who helped transform the Manhattan landscape of the 1980's, is the classic American success story, the American dream realized. F. Scott Fitzgerald would have been fascinated by the Trump story, a Jay Gatsby who actually succeeded (and without the shady past). It can be argued that the acquisition of The Plaza was what gave this hard-working, striving developer true stature, even legitimacy — the construction business version of marrying into royalty.

With Horatio Algerian determination and a ton of greenbacks, Trump's purchase of The Plaza was a triumph of American capitalism and of American social fluidity. It was also a verification of the hotel's genuine democratic roots. People always knew that anyone who had the cash could check into the hotel, now they realized that anyone with the cash could own it too. Trump paid some $400 million for this lucrative piece of property in 1988 and this Prince of Capitalism said he did so knowing he paid too much for it. But we all know how costly dreams can be.

"I would say that the first time I went to The Plaza, I was about seven years old and I went with my parents and we had lunch at the Palm Court one Sunday," Donald Trump confided to me in an interview in 1993, during his tenure as Plaza owner. He was speaking from far back in his swivel chair in his office on the 36th floor of the glass and steel office/apartment tower that so conspicuously bears his name just down the street from The Plaza at 56th and Fifth.

"I just remember the feeling of opulence. There's something very haunting and magical about The Plaza. I don't know what it is. Maybe it's like remnants of the old days. That's why, when I restored the hotel, I wanted to keep it in the same style. I wanted that same feeling." Trump was talking about his lifelong love affair with The Plaza Hotel, but it could almost have been a younger Conrad Hilton remembering his initial fascination.

Trump was especially proud, he continued, that *Condé Nast Traveler* had "rated The Plaza the best business hotel in America. So you know, there are a lot of different ratings and I'm happy about the one we got.

"Hey, Carolyn, can I have a coffee and a diet coke, please," Trump requested, briefly interrupting his train of thought. "When I took The Plaza over it was a mess. And, constantly, you have to work on the hotel because it's not easy to keep up. But it really worked out well. It's doing well and I've restructured the debt, which has been fantastic, where 1 owe 51 percent and essentially I sold 49 percent to a group of institutions. So, I sold debt for equity. I swapped out debt for equity and you know I have total control. I run it but I have institutional partners, which is great because I'm paying a lot less interest."

(Just before Trump bought The Plaza for something in the neighborhood of $400 million — the figure quoted in various reports elsewhere ranged between $390 and $425 million — there was a big rumor things were so bad that the security department was on the verge of telling staffers to clean out their personal effects lockers.)

"But the hotel is doing great. It's making a lot of money," he added.

"Are you still as involved with the running of the hotel as you were?" I asked.

"I decorated most of the public areas myself," he said. "The hallways, the ballrooms, things like that. They were done by me. Ivana did some of the rooms and suites and she had these high-style decorators come in that were all PR and no substance. But we've changed that and the place is incredible."

Trump actually offered $50 million for the hotel in the early 1980's, Philip Hughes, a former longtime Plaza manager, reports. But his offer was flatly rebuffed by the Westin Hotel chain as inadequate.

"This is Westin's flagship (hotel) and we want to keep it in the company," Hughes told the mighty developer. For argument's sake, Trump responded, what would the company take for it? "I called him back and said $100 million and to make a long story short we didn't sell it to Donald."

As Hughes told it, he and The Donald used to have breakfast together every several weeks for about a year.

"You know, I'm going to buy this hotel?" Hughes said The Donald first told him in 1976. "How much would you pay for it?" Hughes asked him. "Twenty-five million," Hughes said Trump responded. "We had only had the hotel for about a year in 1976 and I told him that was what we had paid for it. Immediately Trump said $50 million and I called the chief legal guy for Westin in Seattle and told him Donald Trump was offering $50 million for The Plaza. He said, 'No. And who's Donald Trump?'"

In those days, thirty-six floors below the windows of his command center at Trump Tower, the doors of The Plaza still glistened brightly in the sunlight. But the economic downward slide of the early 1990's took its toll on The Plaza Hotel. Not because occupancy was down. Quite the contrary. Trump, as glamorous a figure as the early-day robber barons who built The Plaza, injected tremendous new life into the hotel.

But the simple fact was he had paid too much for it and was having problems meeting his debt obligations while maintaining the aging giant. Simultaneously, Trump's marriage to Ivana was unravelling the way The Plaza's carpets are never permitted to (at least not for long).

On April 10 1991, Trump, saddled with mounting renovation costs, announced he intended to turn a large portion of The Plaza Hotel's rooms (or as many as he could sell) into condominiums.

The Gannett News Service backed up this story by reporting that "Developer Donald Trump said he would convert most of the swank Plaza Hotel into luxurious condominiums, a move that could cost his ex-wife, Ivana, her job running the posh

Fifth Avenue landmark. . . . A conversion could bring Trump about $750 million, nearly double the $390 million he paid for the hotel three years ago and comes at a time when Trump is under pressure from his bank lenders to sell assets and generate cash."

On Business World, ABC News' Sunday morning show, the veteran news anchor, Sander Vanocur, at the start of the program stated the dilemma succinctly: "If The Plaza Hotel becomes a condo, would Eloise still want to stay there?"

The media message was clear — The Plaza was not just any old piece of property. It belonged to the city, and people cared about it, felt protective of it.

Short, powerfully-built Plaza banquet department executive Bobby D'Angelo, who first began work in the hotel as elevator operator in 1958 when he was 18 years old, nevertheless gives Donald Trump credit for saving The Plaza and Ivana Trump for upgrading service and other amenities.

"If Donald didn't buy this hotel there would have been a lot of people who would have been without a job because at that time the rooms were only 46 percent occupied," he explains.

When D'Angelo first started there were a lot more "permanent" guests living at the hotel, like there are at The Pierre Hotel or Carlyle Hotel today.

While Trump had appointed his wife, Ivana, president of The Plaza, she was much more than the wife of a mogul with a fancy title. Ivana was really a working chief executive. She upgraded the food and restaurants and designed many of the rooms. (She'd also designed suites in Trump's Atlantic City properties.)

"Ivana was very nice, very demanding, very strict and she wanted everything just so," says D'Angelo, who was administrative secretary in the banquet department when I talked to him. His job included doing a lot of the paperwork for the department, as well as booking waiters for various banquets.

"She wanted new plates in the banquet department and made a number of other changes to make the hotel more competitive with other properties."

Mrs. Trump could also be a stickler for details.

"Joe would come and tell stories how Ivana would look down from her apartment in Trump Tower (a few blocks further down Fifth Avenue) — I guess through binoculars — so she could see the Fifth Avenue door of the hotel," Joe Szorentini's wife Veronica recollects. And if she'd spot something she'd call Joe, 'There's paper on the sidewalk, get it cleaned up!'"

"Mrs. Trump would like to walk the Seventh Floor."

This is the type of message that would emanate from the Executive Office of The Plaza when Mrs. Trump wanted to tour a particular floor. It would instill the fear of God into even the most veteran Plaza employees.

The Plaza Pulse, an in-house newsletter, talked about such a stroll down those long, exquisite hallways:

"In preparation for the floorwalk, all of the rooms are placed out of order, so that the Front Office will not see any of them for the day. That morning, the team assembles on the floor, along with the room attendants, housemen and supervisors from that floor. When Mrs. Trump steps off the elevator, armed with tape recorder and a pair of flat shoes, she unleashes a bright smile and a 'good morning, kids' as she bee-lines for the first room at the end of the corridor. We all have to pick up our steps in order to keep up with her. A floorwalk can take anywhere from two to four hours."

From the moment she and Donald took over the hotel, it was literally a hands-on job for Ivana. "Ivana showed how the rooms should be cleaned properly. And it really was more than teaching the guest-room attendants how to clean the bathrooms," explains Richard Wilhelm, The Plaza's general manager during the first several years Trump owned the hotel. "It wasn't really teaching the attendants how to clean the tubs. It was about her espirit de corps. About the fact she really cared for this hotel. It isn't about sitting in an office and barking orders. It's about getting out and around the property and showing there was a real desire of the new ownership and a pride."

Donald and Ivana also had a positive impact on the banquet bottom line, which had been languishing. That Fall, Yasmin Kahn, a friend of Ivana's, was married at The Plaza, setting a tone of lavishness that has continued right through the wedding last year (Nov. 2000) of Michael Douglas and Catherine Zeta-Jones. There were a hundred violinists on the stairs leading to the Grand Ballroom, fifty on each side, as the wedding party and their guests went up to the Grand Ballroom. At the entrance to the reception was a carved ice mountain cascading with beluga caviar.

But no amount of tub and sidewalk cleaning could save The Plaza from its mountainous debt.

Richard D. Nylton wrote in a lengthy piece in *The New York Times* on April 25, 1991, "the empire that Trump built is about to be dismantled." That the banks Trump owed money to supported him and didn't pull the plug on his tottering empire was as much testimony to his defiant courage as to The Plaza's asset value. But, at the time, the situation was dicey indeed.

While it had been snatched from the jaws of fiscal death time and time again, in 1992 the hotel officially went bankrupt. No matter how Trump promoted the hotel to increase its occupancy, which he certainly did, its accumulated debt, coupled with the extraordinarily high cost of maintaining and renovating the 1907 building, The Plaza plunged through the safety net of goodwill that had always managed to save it through the Great Depression and lean days during World War II when Uncle Sam and his men in uniform got cut-rate rooms. And with bankers increasingly calling the shots for The Plaza in 1992, manager Wilhelm put into motion the first steps of its sale three years later.

"I really projected out that The Plaza would have a potential worth of $1 billion but the economy slowed and suddenly

Trump's $425 million purchase price started to be deflated to a $600 million asset in the year 2000," Wilhelm explains.

Furthermore, the Trumps' marriage was coming to an end just at The Donald was trying to improve the hotel. In her book, *The Best Is Yet to Come*, Ivana discussed the breakup:

"My family and I were on our annual post-Christmas ski vacation in Aspen, Colorado, in the last days of 1989, when I became aware that my husband was carrying on an extramarital affair. Donald, the children, and I were having lunch at a restaurant called Bonnie's, which is about halfway down Ajax Mountain; apparently, so was his mistress. Just as we were leaving, I became aware of her presence —

"On February 11, my husband and I formally and legally separated. It was three days before Valentine's Day, a week before my birthday. I would be forty-one. The New York *Post* carried a picture of myself and my then-husband made to look as if it had been torn apart, with a one-word headline: SPLIT . . . "

Trump's wedding to actress Marla Maples in December 1993, which some called the "wedding of the decade," was not so much a wedding, but an affirmation. It affirmed that The Donald, who both *The New York Times* and *The Wall Street Journal* had figured was going down for the final count financially two years before was standing by the woman who he said had stuck by him.

"You have to remember who the loved ones [friends] were and who were not," the bridegroom said in an interview with News 1, a New York TV news channel.

There were 1700 guests invited to Donald and Marla's wedding, which served 10,000 shrimp, 2,000 racks of lamb and 10,000 squab breasts. It had been more than five years since Marla in 1990 told the New York *Post* that her affair with Donald Trump proved to be "THE BEST SEX I EVER HAD." But, the notorious Long Island Railroad or "L.I.R.R." shootings, Trump announced, made him realize that "life is short and I want to do this [get married] now."

Plaza executive chef Bruno Tison had the task of orchestrating the wedding party for Trump and Marla Maples. "Of course, one week was a little short," he told me. "We often put on these kinds of parties in two weeks and in the months of October, November and December, which are the busiest at The Plaza Hotel. We are of course fully staffed and are turned to these kinds of parties. But Mr. Trump's wedding was really beautiful and we had lots of fun."

Less than two years later, news that Trump was quietly shopping The Plaza made bigger headlines than marrying Marla.

"The early 1990s was a tough time in New York. The market was down and to maintain an asset which has probably been undercapitalized for years was extremely difficult," says Plaza asset manager Paul Underhill, who first was associated with The Plaza in the early 1990's when he was responsible for reviewing Plaza operations for the group of banks which were the hotel's biggest creditors and still maintains his position today.

Despite the millions Trump sunk into renovating The Plaza, it badly needed overhauling of much of its back-of-the-house infrastructure such as pumping, roofing and the like, work which had been postponed previously.

And despite their divorce, the Trumps, in their own way, had done as much or more for the hotel as Conrad Hilton had years before.

"Like our new ownership who have been incredibly supportive the Trumps were very supportive as well," explains Tom Civitano, The Plaza's vice-president of sales and marketing. "Ivana was a great ambassador for the time we worked together and Donald used his flair to win guests' loyalty and on certain occasions would even volunteer to speak at their events."

So the bumpy if entertaining Trump-Plaza era was over, like the eerily similar, equally doomed Hilton episode decades earlier. Both owners had been dreaded by the staff, both had proven the staff mostly wrong, both had had trouble with their blonde wives, and both men checked out while the checking out was good.

Plaza Movies — At Home, But Not Alone

For years, films ran regularly at Cinema 3 in the basement of the hotel, but there were almost as many blockbusters being filmed upstairs, and almost as regularly.

Cary Grant, who once filmed a part of Hitchcock's classic *North by Northwest* at The Plaza, once also caused a major ruckus there one morning. Grant loudly and repeatedly started asking where the fourth half of his English muffin was. The Plaza's custom, at that time, was to serve only three halves. After getting no satisfactory answer from the tongue-tied waiter, an assistant manager and even room service, Grant charged downstairs to ask the chef himself. "What did you do with the fourth half?" Grant demanded. Flabbergasted, but ever so politely, the chef replied, "We use it for the fourth base of Eggs Benedict." Grant simmered down, possibly seeing the humor of his overreaction.

But the next time Grant ordered an English muffin, and every time thereafter, it came with four halves.

It could easily have been a scene from one of Grant's classic screwball comedies, most of which took place in elegant surroundings much like The Plaza. But it was not fiction, it was just another movie-star episode at The Plaza.

The Plaza scenes from *North by Northwest*, which was released in 1959, were shot in the Oak Bar and the Central Park South lobby. However, the hotel room scene, where Grant tries to find out who he's been mistaken for, was shot on a Hollywood sound stage.

In *Evenings With Cary Grant*, Nancy Nelson relates that the film star was uneasy at the outset about the fate of *North by Northwest*. The sequences shot in The Plaza especially worried the star because of their humor. During production he was afraid his character was more like David Niven than his own famously debonair self.

In 1974, Suite 803 of The Plaza was featured in *The Great Gatsby* starring Robert Redford and Mia Farrow. The scene was not filmed at The Plaza, but in Pinewood Studios. However, The Plaza was nonetheless in the scene: The guest room door numbers, along with six pieces of gold-washed silver plated flatware, thirty-two dinner plates and ashtrays with matchbox holders and many other items were shipped by The Plaza over to the British studios for the filming.

Suites that actually were used by Hollywood include 723, for *Plaza Suite*, starring Walter Matthau, Lee Grant, Eli Wallach and Anne Jackson, and 449 in *Barefoot in the Park* starring Jane Fonda and Robert Redford.

Redford has had quite an association with The Plaza. He also stayed at the hotel while filming *The Way We Were* with singer and all-around-superstar Barbra Streisand. She, in fact, was in the penthouse suite of the hotel while filming the movie, but due to her popularity had registered downstairs as Katie Morosley, her character in the film.

For *Barefoot*, released in 1967, director Gene Saks also used the forth floor corridor of the hotel for one scene as well as the 59th street lobby. For *Crocodile Dundee*, shot in 1986, most of The Plaza scenes were done at the hotel with a lot of the cast and crew put up at the hotel.

Not that there hasn't been the occasional dud on The Plaza's film roster. Along with the *Arthurs*, *The Great Gatsbys* and the *North by Northwests*, has been, for example, *Ma and Pa Kettle Go to Town*. Filmed in 1950, critics across the country went to town panning it. *Love at First Bite*, starring George Hamilton in a humorous take on Dracula, an American International Film produced in 1978, was similarly bled dry by the critical establishment.

※

New York journalist Stephen Silverman once conducted a memorable interview at The Plaza with Bette Davis:

"Now we must be careful what we say about The Plaza," Davis, wafting her cigarette smoke up into one of the hotel's famously lofty ceilings, cautioned Silverman. "'You know,' she said with impeccable diction, 'they've tried very hard to get rid of The Plaza. (Down went her hand on a table). That would be the end of New York.'"

Silverman has also interviewed Liza Minnelli, in The Palm Court, where the entire cast of her first film *The Sterile Cuckoo* (her first starring role) sang the title song "Come Get Under Morning." It was also the setting used for "People" from *Funny Girl*. Then there was the time he showed up at Fifth and Fifty-ninth to gamely try to interview *Star Wars* star Carrie Fisher while she was prone in bed with a bad cold. He ended up prescribing a doctor.

※

The filming of *Home Alone 2*, starring Macaulay Culkin, began in December 1991 and lasted for weeks. To try to help make guests who had nothing to do with the filming feel part of it, and at the same time weather the inconveniences, The Plaza parceled out 3,000 videocassettes of *Home Alone*, the original movie.

And, like Eloise decades before, this second famous Plaza brat paid off big-time for the hotel publicity-wise.

"What it's done for The Plaza in terms of family market is incredible. Combine *Home Alone 2* and *Eloise*, The Plaza may have the two most recognized children's characters in any setting outside a theme park. The Plaza has always been a magical experience for children and this movie underscored that point to a generation of viewers," said Tom Civitano, Vice President of Sales and Marketing.

Speaking of films in general, Civitano adds, "This is not something that just arrives at our doorstep. We actively solicit this type of business. The movies and television shows are as much a part of The Plaza as its celebrity guests."

According to Plaza historian Curtis Gathje, The Plaza had appeared in no less than 34 major feature films by the year 2000.

But only the filming of *Home Alone 2* prompted a major alteration in the hotel's decor. In his book At The Plaza, Gathje relates that one sequence required "Culkin to slide across the floor into a waiting elevator. To make the stunt possible, the film crew had been given permission to remove the wall-to-wall carpeting, in place at that time for about 25 years. When owner Donald Trump saw the exquisite mosaic-tile floor that lay underneath, he was so taken by it that wall-to-wall carpeting was banned thereafter, in favor of area rugs that allowed the mosaics to be seen again."

Every time *Home Alone 2* is shown on TV, The Plaza and the Fairmont Hotels reservations system get several hundred calls for rooms. Some callers even request suite 411, the room "in" the movie. But since the decor of the real 411 is much different than that of its cinematic doppelganger, guests are often asked if they'll take other similar accommodations.

※

If *Home Alone 2* caused some inconvenience and consternation from some Plaza guests during the weeks sequences were being shot at The Plaza, Marilyn Monroe's very presence in a revealing black velvet dress — and a bit out of it — made headlines across the globe when on February 9, 1956 she and costar Laurence Olivier held a press conference to promote their new film, *The Prince and the Showgirl*, based on the Terrence Rattigan play *The Sleeping Prince*.

After taking off her jacket and leaning forward a bit, Monroe, then at the very apex of her fame — and voluptuousness — broke her left shoulder strap amid gasps from even the most blase reporters and paparazzi in attendance. The next second the room practically ignited from flashbulbs. After getting a safety pin to tie the strap in place, it — darn it — broke again! It was all a cleverly conceived publicity stunt for the movie. Olivier, who was in on the gag, piped up, "Shall I take off my coat, boys? Does anybody care?"

The biggest concern Plaza managers had about Marilyn's staged strap snapping incident was not whether the top of her dress would come off but that her dress would fly up. "She didn't wear underclothes. Never," one hotel source who became a Monroe friend but was never romantically involved with the sexy superstar told me. "When they made that movie where her dress flew up they had to make her wear underclothes. But she didn't want to wear them."

❋

Richard Burton and Elizabeth Taylor stayed at The Plaza February 3-8, 1968, to publicize their new movie *Dr. Faustus* (which was roundly panned). The couple was at the height of their tabloid popularity. If there was a flurry of activity inside the hotel, even with the staff specially instructed to always address Miss Taylor as Mrs. Richard Burton, there was near pandemonium outside. Legendary Hollywood publicist John Springer, who represented "The Burtons" at the time, told me, "The crowd outside the hotel was huge and Richard used to put my son, Gary, who was a little boy at the time, up on his shoulders and they got caught in the crowd and Gary came back without any shoes. They were grabbing at anything they could get their hands on, including my sons shoes!"

Based on the legend of Faust, who sells his soul to Mephistopheles, the story of the poetry-rich Dr. Faustus (a stage version of which he and Taylor had already done at Oxford University) was symbolic of the turning point in Burton's own life. Having triumphed in *Hamlet* on Broadway several years earlier, one of the greatest actors of his generation had become a son of Hollywood, faithful to its glories and indulgences, including his gift to Taylor of a pigeon-egg–sized 69.42 carat Cartier diamond.

The couple encamped with regal Hollywood splendor into the Plaza's Royal Suite, 1401-7, with six bedrooms and the sixth, room 1407, exclusively "to be used for Mrs. Burton's clothes," according to an internal hotel memo at the time just prior to their arrival. The same memo highlighted Mr. Burton's penchant for strong drink. It said: "Mr. Burton will require Johnny Walker Red Label, Noilly Prat Dry Vermouth, Beefeater Gin, Soda, Gingerale.... Dom Perignon Champagne." The words "also Jack Daniels" were inserted at the end of the memo as an urgent afterthought.

At an impromptu press conference, the Burtons were asked some pretty tough questions for the times. Milder, however, was one about star billing directed to Miss Taylor. "I always say I will not accept top billing. And Richard says 'you bloody well WILL accept first billing!'"

"Mr. Burton, have you learned anything from Miss Taylor?" was another question. "Well," began the Welsh actor, grinning, "when we close the door tonight . . . " Whereupon Miss Taylor slapped him. More seriously, he continued, "She's taught me a great deal about film acting."

"Richard says, you are extravagant," another reporter probed. "He says you spend $1000 a minute."

"What a [expletive deleted]!," Mrs. Burton replied. "Why that's cheap. I'm very good about my budget — at times!" One reporter who went to their suite for a private Q&A session, overheard Burton wickedly reply to his wife's query about her choice of attire for an upcoming event — "Why don't you go naked?!"

On a more domestic note, ten-year-old Kate Burton, daughter with Burton's first wife Sybil, joined her dad and new step-mom at The Plaza and Taylor took her shopping at FAO Schwartz.

※

Like the late legendary actor Anthony Quinn and gossip columnist Cindy Adams, Jack Lemmon loved Trader Vic's. But the jut-jawed Lemmon, a two-time Academy Award winner and veteran of over fifty films, was so much an Everyman that he often went unrecognized as he dined on fried shrimp and the restaurant's more exotic Polynesian fare.

※

At the height of their fame as a couple and actors, Melanie Griffith and husband Don Johnson used to stay at The Plaza under an assumed name, Mr. and Mrs. Richard Head, informed Plaza sources have informed me. One evening they were coming home from a party and Melanie, who was in a jovial mood, yelled over to one Plaza employee she recognized, 'Hi! It's Mr. and Mrs. Dick Head!!" The red-faced employee greeted them warmly as if she has said "Mr. and Mrs. Jane."

※

Like he did everywhere else, Frank Sinatra did it his "his way" at The Plaza. Once, when Sinatra had requested a meeting with one of the hotel managers, the superstar opened his hotel room door stark naked, a manager told me.

"'Mr. Sinatra, don't you think you should get some clothes on?' the manager said he asked the chairman of the board, then turned to leave. "'I wanted to talk to you about something and you leave when I say so,'" the manager said Sinatra replied. "Mr. Sinatra, why don't you have your secretary call me after you're dressed and we can discuss the whole matter,'" the manager concluded.

In later years, Sinatra rented Cole Porter's old suite (33A) in The Waldorf Towers at a cost of nearly $1 million a year, according to sources at The Waldorf. The Chairman of the Board also liked to stay in the penthouse of The Fontainebleau (now the Fontainebleau Hilton) when he was in Miami. "He was free and easy with old-time entertainers. He'd give them a couple hundred bucks," one hotel source confided to me.

Mia Farrow first met Frank Sinatra at a private screening of *None But the Brave*, she says in her autobiography *Mia Farrow: What Falls Away* and the singer immediately invited her to his Palm Springs estate for the weekend. They jet-setted around the globe and attended Truman Capote's Black and White Ball at The Plaza on November 28, 1966, before they were married the following year. According to daughter Nancy Sinatra's book, *Frank Sinatra: An American Legend*, Sinatra told Nancy on July 19, 1966, just prior to marrying Mia, that "I don't know, maybe we'll only have a couple of years together. She's so young. But we have to try."

"Once when I took Stevie Wonder to his suite — he usually stayed in the same corner Plaza suite on the park — he stopped suddenly and said, 'Something's different.' former manager Richard Wilhelm related me. "'I know. You're asking yourself how I know something is different. I can't see. I can smell the difference! It's cleaner!'"

Actress Rosalind Russell couldn't have had a more charismatic host than Jack Benny to present her with the Tenth Annual Floyd B. Odlum Award for her work for the Arthritis Foundation in the mid-1960s at the hotel. Then Benny reverted to type with his remarks about hosting the event so he could save the $50 dinner fee.

Marlene Dietrich checked into The Plaza for more than a year starting in early 1948 shortly after making *A Foreign Affair* and while she awaited the birth of her first grandchild. "The four-room apartment came equipped with mirrored walls, an ornate red antique French clock, and bedroom murals of frolicking nymphs hand-painted by the artist Marcel Vertes," according to the book *At The Plaza*.

Even at age 62 in 1962, Dietrich had a figure even high fashion models envied. Famed columnist and public relations guru Eleanor Lambert recalled being shocked to see how slim Dietrich was and how good she looked in a practically nude see-through body stocking when the two were trying out designer clothes that same year. It was even harder for her neighbors at The Plaza to figure how the superstar kept her weight in check given the lusty aromatic German cooking including wieners and bratwurst she liked to do in her suite.

One of the saddest recorded visits of a star to The Plaza was Playmate-of-the-Year Dorothy Straten's to filmmaker Peter Bogdonovich's suite in the summer of 1980 — Suite 1001, Bogdonovich writes in his book on Straten, *The Killing of the Unicorn*. Ostensibly, Straten, who had a part in the director's movie *They All Laughed*, was staying at the Wyndham Hotel on West 58th Street across from The Plaza. But Paul Snider, the man who "discovered" her for *Playboy* and killed her on August 14, 1980, in a fit of jealous rage, had hired photographers to tail her to New York and prove she and Bogdonovich were living together.

"One morning, there was a knock on the door of the suite," Bogdonovich writes. "D.R. (his name for Dorothy Straten) went to answer, thinking it was room service. She didn't check the peephole, so the door of 1001 opened onto a pair of photographers Snider had sent to find her . . . How had they known she was there? Dorothy hadn't asked . . . Although they had said the Wyndham staff had told them to try Bogdonovich's suite at The Plaza, it was more likely the information had come through detectives Snider had retained . . . Soon we would hear that Snider was going around the mansion (the Playboy mansion) telling everyone who would listen that Dorothy had run off with Bogdonovich, and they were shacked up together at The Plaza." Snider killed her in LA later that same summer.

Two-time Oscar nominee Sylvia Miles was married in 1963 in the hotel's second floor "state suite," comprised of several function rooms which used to be leased out living quarters. But unlike Eddie Murphy and his bride and Michael Douglas and Catherine Zeta-Jones, who spent their honeymoon nights at the hotel, Miles and radio personality Ted Brown went back to Miles' apartment in The Osborne, an historic apartment house on 57th Street and Seventh Avenue which predates The Plaza.

"The honeymoon was longer than the marriage," joked Miles, a great screen and stage actress and good friend. Miles has long since moved to Central Park South but says, "I stay at The Plaza every time I have a movie to promote. I ask the film company to put me up at The Plaza. It's like my second home!"

The Beatles, Neil Simon, and Other Artists

The Beatles came, they stayed, they conquered. They even won over the staff of The Plaza — an audience not easily impressed. They arrived at The Plaza February 7, 1964 and stayed for six days. Their reservations were made under their real names which, because they were largely unknown in this country, didn't alert the operator that a tidal wave of teens was about to descend on the grand hotel. The Beatles stayed in suites, 1260, 1263, 1264, and 1273, all small suites in 1964, and were on the 58th Street side of the hotel "so they wouldn't be as noticeable if they looked out the window" one internal memo noted.

They appeared on *The Ed Sullivan Show* Sunday night, and had back-to-back concerts at nearby Carnegie Hall Wednesday, February 12th. They also partied at the Peppermint Lounge on West 45th Street and The Playboy Club, which was then across Fifth Avenue from The Plaza. When they returned to the U.S. in August 1964, they stayed at the Delmonico Hotel. Still, The Plaza was where everyone supposed they *would* stay, and in poured letters asking the management to send them anything the Beatles touched.

"Dear Sir, If the Beatles stay at your hotel please send me

some of their cigarette butts. Please?!" one Illinois girl wrote. Alphonse W. Salomone replied, briefly, "I have your letter but regret that I cannot help. The Beatles are not staying at The Plaza in this visit to the city."

But this in itself caused a huge roar as many letters poured in criticizing The Plaza for banning the "gold bugs," as they were also being dubbed. "I read you canceled the reservation for [the Beatles] second trip to America," one irate young woman wrote. "Were you afraid the girls would gather around your establishment? They might hurt a bush or something?"

It wasn't bushes but concern over safety. Some half dozen teenage girls were injured during the melee of the group's first visit in February and the hotel's security force had to be upped from the normal 60 to 150.

Bobby D'Angelo, who has been in The Plaza banquet department since the time the Beatles stayed there, remembers, "at that time they were really new so you didn't know what was going on. But you knew it was something that was going to take off. They came in on February 7, 1964 and they stayed about five days. They went to *The Ed Sullivan Show* and I served them breakfast one morning and I remember that Ringo [Starr] was a comic. He used to kid around. HE was the outspoken one. I was a banquet waiter at the time. I served them breakfast in the baroque suite, a banquet room — all the way down the end of the hall at the very far west end of the hotel.

"They had a lot of publicity people," he continued. "They had disc jockeys that were here. They were all with them and their publicist. All their entourage. They were nice to serve, though. They were regular people. They weren't demanding or anything."

Although the Beatles were virtually unknown to many at The Plaza when they arrived, the whirlwind impact of their celebrity was so great that some of the waiters found themselves actually copying the Beatle pageboy hairstyles. But The Beatles' appearance on the *Ed Sullivan Show* had a much more profound affect on the nation, said George Harrison in *The Beatles Anthology*: "I've heard that while the Beatles were on there were no reported crimes."

"After a couple of months I realized how famous they were getting. I said to myself, 'I wish I had gotten their autographs,'" D'Angelo continues. "I've served so many famous people it's incredible. I've served Tony Bennett, Frank Sinatra. Frank Sinatra was a sport. You take care of him and he takes care of you. Not cheap at all. He'll give you a $100 tip like it was nothing. (Contrary to the above-stated opinion.)

"And he gave a lot, a whole lot to charity you never knew about. That was class. I respect that."

William H. Carr, a former night city editor of the New York *Post*, and the author of many books including the best-selling *The Duponts of Delaware*, says he went to The Plaza to visit old friend Jan Dupont when the Beatles were in residence.

"I went to visit her and have dinner and I saw this crowd and I hadn't realized the Beatles were staying there, though there were thousands of people. They had gathered in the Pulitzer Fountain area on the Fifth Avenue side of The Plaza. They were spilling over into Fifth Avenue and the cops were having trouble keeping them out of Fifth Avenue. Just an unbelievable mass of teenagers, and as I fought my way through, I also found it a very funny thing because the manager had politely said to Jan, who had been staying there for years, 'I'm sure you won't mind moving to another floor (other than the 12th floor where the Beatles were staying). They need a whole floor for themselves.' And Jan said to him, 'I certainly *would* mind!' And she stayed right on the same floor with them."

The Beatles' six days at The Plaza pushed guests and staff either to nervous exhaustion, delirium, capitulation, or a dizzying combination of all three. Beleaguered Plaza telephone switchboard operators had the added burden of deciphering what calls to switch to Ringo, John, George and Paul and which to detour to the publicity department, which fielded the bulk of them.

A special phone code — a precursor of sorts to modern-day credit card numbers — was devised and no calls were routed to the Beatles when unaccompanied by this code. Nevertheless, overzealous reporters, TV producers, ad men and hucksters alike, some of whom claimed they were relatives, besieged the switchboard with hundreds of urgent but unrequited phone calls.

But there were relatively few complaints from other guests considering many couldn't place phone calls since the hotel's operators were so busy fielding calls from fans.

Things did get out of hand when one hotel employee, one of publicist Eve Brown's assistants, was desperately trying to reach the Beatles' manager Brian Epstein by phone and couldn't get through. She raced up to the Beatles' twelfth floor suite where she was outraged to see one of the photographers snapping pictures of a Beatle jumping on the bed in his room — and coaching him to go ever higher.

"Shocked and horrified, she turned on the lensman with the full force of her Irish temper. 'How dare you do this to The Plaza? Why are you manufacturing these sensational pictures? This boy is probably afraid not to go along with the press, and just look what he's doing to our beautiful satin covers. Nobody acts this way at The Plaza, nobody, not even the Beatles. Now you stop this nonsense this very minute.'" Eve Brown wrote.

"As gentle applause issued from newsmen who had been observing from the sidelines, the photographer, crushed beneath the fine fury, quickly slunk away."

The Beatles Anthology, the history of the Beatles which proudly proclaims it's "by the Beatles," clears up one mystery about the group's stay at The Plaza. George Harrison was conspicuously absent when John, Ringo and Paul waded through the throngs outside the hotel to go into Central Park to do publicity shots. Harrison confesses in *The Beatles* that "I had a bad throat and that's why I'm missing . . . The same with the rehearsal for Ed Sullivan: there are pictures of them rehearsing without me. I could never figure out how, with swarms of people everywhere, with the mania going on, they actually did get out into the park for a photo session."

But this much is certain: The Beatles reveled in the crowds, New York, and The Plaza. "I loved New York at that time," writes Ringo. "We went into Central Park in a horse-drawn carriage. We had this huge suite of rooms in The Plaza Hotel, with a TV in every room, and we had radios with earpieces. This was all so fascinating to me. It was too far out; the media was just so fast.

"I remember that on one of the TV channels they were showing *Hercules Unchained*, an Italian toga and sandal epic. When we got up in the morning and put the TV on there would be Hercules doing his stuff in ancient times. We'd go out and do something and come back in the afternoon and I'd switch on and he would *still* be doing his stuff. And then we'd go out at night and come back, and I'd switch on this one channel, and it would be the same movie! I thought I was cracking up. In fact, this one channel had a Movie of the Week, and they would just keep showing it again and again. At the end of the credits they'd just start it at the top.

"This was just too far out, coming from England, where we'd only had a TV in our house for a couple of years. Now here was a channel doing something crazy like this."

If F. Scott Fitzgerald is the 20th Century novelist people most often associate with The Plaza, playwright Neil Simon has made the hotel a permanent fixture on Broadway. And Simon, old enough to have grown up in an era when elegance was still as popular an American pastime as sex and violence on TV seem to be these days, is one of the long line of this century's most successful writers to call The Plaza home, as well as his personal Muse.

Aside from his current hit *The Dinner Party*, his *Lost in Yonkers* won the 1991 Pulitzer prize for Drama and the Tony Award for Best Play. His first Broadway play, *Come Blow Your Horn*, produced in 1959, was only a moderate success yet still ran for two years. His second effort, *Barefoot in the Park* was a blockbuster and his career took off. Perhaps it was only coincidence that part of the play takes place at The Plaza, but in any case, Simon's phenomenal, long-running success and his literary treatments of the hotel began at the same instant.

I talked to Simon in his New York apartment in the building where he once lived with his second wife, actress Marsha Mason.

Such was the success of *Barefoot in the Park* that "I was blown away by it," Simon explained. "It was just so enormous. So I said to myself, 'Is this what a hit feels like?'"

As a young boy I can vividly remember seeing the play during a matinee performance. Simon's newlyweds were played by Robert Redford and Elizabeth Ashley, and when actress Mildred Natwick entered their apartment, teetering and wheezing after laboring up seven flights of stairs, the audience broke out into seemingly uncontrollable laughter.

In *Barefoot in the Park* the newlyweds honeymoon at The Plaza and later go barefoot in Central Park so Robert Redford's stuffy lawyer character can learn a gentle lesson about loosening up. Years later, in *Plaza Suite*, which is really three one-act plays, Simon used the hotel as a backdrop for more serious themes, to discuss weddings and infidelity.

Harvey Sabinson, a former Broadway press agent who became executive director of the League of American Theatres and Producers, told me that when he at one time worked as Simon's personal press agent, Simon and his producer were all prepared to call the new play *Waldorf Suite*, if The Plaza had balked at Simon using their name.

But Simon doesn't remember it that way: "It may have been on the film. That's what may have happened. I have no recollection about it for the play. Of course, I've forgotten a lot of things that have happened.

"I do remember this about The Plaza. I was living on 62nd Street, I believe at the time. And they were painting my house. I said, 'I need to go and work,' because I wanted to finish *The Gingerbread Lady*.

"So I went over to The Plaza and I said, 'Do you have a small room to work in?' They said, 'Yes, we do.' And they gave me a room that was virtually a maid's room. So I had my typewriter there. And I could send up for room service. I spent about four weeks there and I would say I wrote a majority of that play in The Plaza."

"I also spent my honeymoon night at The Plaza with Joan. But what made me think of The Plaza Hotel for *Plaza Suite*? Because I could have picked another hotel to write about. I could have said, 'Waldorf Suite' or something. But The Plaza to me had the most class. It also predated the Waldorf by a long time. So there was something about that hotel I thought was very romantic whereas I didn't feel that about the other hotels.

"Mike Nichols and I had a problem with *Plaza Suite* and it was a strange problem. We had done *Barefoot in the Park* together and we had done *The Odd Couple*. And we played them both in Boston and they were huge hits and then we showed up there with *Plaza Suite* and they said, 'Neil Simon and Mike Nichols. It will be a big comedy hit.' So we do that first act about the husband and wife breaking up after twenty-three years and they were laughing. There were places for them to laugh but then it got serious — but they were laughing. So Mike said to me. 'We have to take out all these little laughs because it's hurting the drama in the piece.' I think they were laughing at the identification; husbands and wives going through this. The vanity of a man turning fifty and trying to look younger or maybe having an affair with the secretary.

"The general manager of our play said, 'Neil, you're going to get into a lot of trouble with all the people who come from out of town and go to a play with some girl. They're going to see their lives up there.' I said, 'that's not my job to worry about those people. If I can put the truth up on stage, that's what I want to do.'"

In *Plaza Suite* there are some poignant lines about the changing skyline of New York. In the play, the character played by Maureen Stapleton tells her husband that the last time they stayed in the suite their view was altogether different.

Simon was actually pointing out a time in the city's history where, "If you went away for a weekend, a building was not there any more." That's what was happening to New York in the 1960's and 1970's.

"When I talk about New York in *Laughter on the 23rd Floor* (in the 1950's) the city was so great. And then they started to tear down things, changing New York."

One of the funniest and most telling exchanges about the ever-changing nature of New York City in *Plaza Suite* occurs when Karen and her husband, Sam, come to the hotel to celebrate their 24th wedding anniversary. Karen asks the bellhop if he's sure the suite she's in is room 719, the same one where she and Sam spent their honeymoon.

The bellhop says, "I'm here for two years. and it's always been 719."

(The dialogue continues:)

KAREN: Because you know about 826 at the Savoy-Plaza?

BELLHOP: No ma'am.

KAREN: Oh, well, they had a famous murder in 826. Then the next year there was a fire and the year after that a husband and wife committed suicide. Then no one wanted 826. So they turned it into a linen closet. In fact, there's no more 826 at the Savoy-Plaza.

BELLHOP: There's no more Savoy Plaza either. They tore it down two years ago.

KAREN: Oh, my God, look at that. There's no Savoy Plaza! What's that monstrosity?

BELLHOP: It's the new General Motors Building.

One thing you can tell is that this scene was certainly written before the era of product endorsements in films.

In a much, much earlier time, the early 1930's, the elderly actor, playwright and producer William Gillette, America's first Sherlock Holmes, wrote (macabrely in red ink) to The Plaza's Hotel Housekeeper to make a most specific request:

"Will you please, if it is possible in these times of depression, have a wide bed put in my room instead of two narrow ones which usually do duty in your apartments. The time is not far off when I shall have to sleep permanently in very narrow quarters and my wish is not to begin any sooner than necessary."

Sixty years later The Plaza got another unusual letter, postmarked in Hong Kong with no address beyond "The Plaza, U.S.A." This, though, was an inside job.

"I had a friend who went on vacation in Hong Kong and I asked him to put 'The Plaza Hotel, United States of America,' on the envelope," confesses Plaza vice-president of sales and marketing Tom Civitano. "And within fourteen days of being postmarked it arrived at The Plaza. I don't know if there are too many hotels in the world which over the years have built such a strong brand recognition that a local postman in a foreign country knew which postal bag to place the letter in to arrive at our address only identified as 'The Plaza.'"

Like Neil Simon and William Gillette, writers and actors have long loved The Plaza, but many, like the Beatles, are placed there by their publicists. Often, when left to their own devices, they stay at a smaller New York hotel such as The Mark or The Lowell. Film star Eric Stoltz stays at The Plaza at his publicist's or movie studio's request. Otherwise he prefers a Manhattan apartment.

For some artists, however, the hotel creates a feeling of well-being that has eluded them in the past. Refugees from totalitarian regimes, for instance.

Playwright Ferenc Molnar, who lived at The Plaza from 1940 to 1952, gave his staff orders never to tell anyone of his whereabouts. After all, he'd been a refugee from the Nazi terror and his Jewish wife, who'd been incarcerated by the Nazis, had suffered terribly.

The Hungraian playwright had only modest success with his drawing room comedy *The Guardsman* until real-life husband and wife stage stars Alfred Lunt and Lynn Fontanne played the witty and jealous husband and wife in a 1924 Broadway production of the play. But Molnar's greatest contribution to the American theater came when he was living at The Plaza. The "book" (or story) of the 1945 Rodgers and Hammerstein musical *Carousel* was based on Molnar's moving fantasy *Liliom* which starred Eva Le Gallienne and Joseph Schildkraut in New York in 1921.

The playwright Maeterlinck also lived at The Plaza during some of Molnar's time there. They were both surprised to find out each other's secret, although it's believed Molnar was the more private of the two.

Jones Harris, offspring of Broadway director Jed Harris and actress Ruth Gordon, recalls once meeting Molnar at The Plaza:

"My father brought me to The Plaza to see Molnar. He had a small, little room or a couple of small rooms and Molnar was a great one for walking. He would literally just walk on that block. It would take him up to Sixth Avenue and there was a wonderful delicatessen that he would go to off Central Park and then he'd continue to walk on that block and come back to the hotel. And, so, he continued on that same block that The Plaza was on. He was not a great one for wandering away from that."

This habit may have been the result of trouble Molnar had earlier in life, as Harris goes on to explain: "When he was a young man in Budapest, there were lots of foot panders (thiefs). And they still had horses and carriages. And he was very nervous about riding in them because he was afraid that a foot pander would jump him. So what he would do was sit in the jump seat of the horsecab and gesticulate with his hands as if he was talking to at least two other people in the dark of the back of the cab, even though there was no one there. So the foot panders, seeing that, thought to themselves there were too many people to try and stop."

Molnar himself once wrote in a 1950 magazine article of The Plaza as "a citadel, a fortress for all of us who live here. After two decades of wandering during which I have stayed in those good but noisy hotels with cardboard walls, any time I come here to this mighty edifice with the wide open free space about it, I have a sense of quiet security, solidity."

New York restaurateur George Lang explains that Molnar was also a member of an informal expatriate roundtable from Hungary that met regularly in the Oak Room. It was started by Alexander Ince who had also started *Stage* magazine. The circle's members, who would come and go, included producers Billy Rose and Gilbert Miller and, from time to time, Al Hirschfeld, the renowned *New York Times* artist.

Going back to the year the hotel opened, world renowned Metropolitan Opera tenor Enrico Caruso, who later moved to the Knickerbocker Hotel on 42nd Street and Broadway for twelve years, checked into a large corner suite to see what all the fuss was about with this newest, most glamorous hotel. As temperamental as he was talented, the tenor had a fit when on December 8, 1907, "the buzzing sound made by the magneta" interrupted his singing practice. Whereupon, Plaza legend has it, the great Caruso charged the gilded magneta clock on the fireplace mantle of his suite with a knife, breaking it and throwing all 245 magneta clocks, which were controlled electronically by one master, out of whack.

Ninety years later when actor Daniel Baldwin allegedly used drugs in his Plaza room, the police were promptly called and led him away in handcuffs. In Caruso's day and case, the hotel management sent him a magnum of champagne to apologize.

※

The Plaza's eeriest "artistic" association — however oblique — was with mother-and-son grifters, Sante and Kenneth Kimes. These of the con artist variety. The pair were convicted in May 2000 of 118 charges for the murder of Upper East Side millionaire Irene Silverman, whose body hadn't been found at the time. The Kimes had checked a black bag at The Plaza with a manila envelope in it which contained the deed to Silverman's East 65th Street townhouse. The chilling words "Final Dynasty" were scribbled on the outside of the envelope.

An almost equally bizarre, if far less ominous, incident occurred in 1986, when an aging and increasingly unsuccessful Bob Fosse reluctantly came to The Plaza to accept the Fred Astaire Award for the best dances on Broadway. As author/drama critic Martin Gottfried writes in his book *The Life and Death of Bob Fosse*, instead of being gracious Fosse castigated the critics for treatment of *Big Deal*, a big Fosse flop, which had closed after a measly 62 performances.

But the worst was yet to come. Fosse companion Phoebe Ungerer suddenly turned on *Daily News* critic Doug Watt, who had panned *Big Deal*, and, according to Gottfried, cried something to which the gentlemanly Watt could only reply, "That's not very ladylike."

※

Architect Frank Lloyd Wright, despite his otherwise noted fondness for the hotel, once sniffed to a reporter that "The Plaza was built by the Astors, Astorists, Plastorbilts and Whoeverbilts who wanted a place to dress up and parade and see themselves in the great mirrors."

One of Wright's biggest clients, S. R. Guggenheim, once occupied The Plaza second floor State Suites, which overlook both Fifth Avenue and Central Park. Guggenheim settled into his suite with a wide array of original Impressionist paintings that included the work of such greats as Chagall, Matisse, Klee and Seurat.

Literary greats from F. Scott Fitzgerald to Dorothy Parker stayed at The Plaza because they liked to entertain and be entertained. In John Keats' book, *You Might as Well Live: The Life and Times of Dorothy Parker*, the author tells how Parker went to The Plaza not only to write, but also because she felt it was a place where she could really find her soul — that there were times when she extended her stays at the hotel to get a whole new lease on life.

As it has been for so many, The Plaza was also the backdrop for a major turning point in Dorothy Parker's career. In her book, *Dorothy Parker: What Fresh Hell is This?* author Marion Meade chronicles a tea at The Plaza in January 1920, during which *Vanity Fair* editor Frank Crowninshield fired Parker from her job writing dramatic criticism because he told her a former staffer was returning to the magazine. The real reason, however, was Parker's blistering criticism of some of the shows produced by some of the biggest names of the day, including Florenz Ziegfeld and David Belasco, who were also major advertisers in *Vanity Fair*.

"After leaving The Plaza, Parker steamed home to telephone [Robert] Benchley, who came into the city on the next train . . . Dorothy's dismissal seemed genuinely unfair and undeserved because she had praised many productions and many performers," Meade writes. But her dismissal also resulted in Parker becoming a successful freelance writer and establishing a bigger name for herself on the *New Yorker* magazine which would be born several years later.

In protest of what he felt was the magazine's shoddy treatment of his friend, Benchley resigned his own post as managing editor, whereupon Parker and Benchley rented a tiny Times Square office to write their freelance assignments.

⊠

In the early 1920's after the roaring success of his first novel, *This Side of Paradise*, Fitzgerald lived in an apartment at 38 West 59th Street between The Plaza and Sixth Avenue, while partying at The Plaza and frequenting its Grill Room.

Fitzgerald also employed the services of a Plaza stenographer at a time in 1922 when he was unable to use his writing hand. The novelist set scenes not only from *The Great Gatsby* at the hotel but *The Beautiful and the Damned*.

Actress Marion Seldes's father, literary critic Gilbert Seldes, was a close Fitzgerald confidante and friend. Marion has said her father shared and understood Fitzgerald's love for The Plaza.

Seldes recalled that the two friends also belonged to a close-knit group. "The group contained my father, Fitzgerald, and my mother, who was a great friend of Zelda's. And, to me, by the time I was old enough to know what that friendship was and what the South of France was like, and what the time was, it was over. I used to think of it as the golden time of my own father's life as well as Fitzgerald's."

Ernest Hemingway, another intimate of Fitzgerald's circle, once advised F. Scott, regarding his friend's future funeral plans, "If you really feel blue enough, get yourself insured and I'll see you can get killed and I'll write a fine obituary. We can take your liver out and give it to the Princeton Museum, your heart to The Plaza Hotel."

Song and dance man George M. Cohan was the biggest entertainer to adopt The Plaza as a hangout. As Bill Harris writes in his picture book on The Plaza, "The Plaza is less than ten minutes from Broadway and it was a convenient place for George M. Cohan to unwind after his day in theater and before the curtain went up on the evening performance. Most days he arrived at 4:00 and went straight to the northwest corner of the Oak Room where he had a table permanently reserved. His business associates knew where to find him, and from four to seven each day, the Oak Room corner was as important a part of the Broadway scene as Times Square itself.

"Some days," Harris continues, Cohan "was more in a

mood for strolling than for planning and reminiscing. When that mood struck him, he went to the cashier's office and bought a roll of quarters, which he dispensed one at a time to folks in Central Park who looked like they could use the money . . . His beneficiaries probably gave him his own curtain line in response: 'My mother thanks you, my father thanks you, my sister thanks you... and *I* thank you!'"

After he died in the early '40's, the Lambs Club put up a plaque on the wall of the Oak Room commemorating the room's "Cohan Corner." Harris said of this honor, "It's a memorial he probably would have loved every bit as much as the statue of himself that was placed in Times Square in just about the same spot that had earlier been proposed for Saint Gaudens' *General Sherman*."

Cohan, immortalized by the 1941 Jimmy Cagney film *Yankee Doodle Dandy*, wrote the classic American songs "Give My Regards to Broadway" and "Over There" (the latter earning him a Congressional Medal of Honor). He dominated the Broadway of the Plaza's first decade with such shows as *Little Johnny Jones* and *Get-Rich-Quick Wallingford*.

Tremendously popular with audiences as a tunesmith, playwright and performer, Cohan, like the modern-day Andrew Lloyd Webber, was not without his detractors. Alexander Woollcott said one Cohan play sounded, "as if he had written it on the back of an envelope while he was waiting for the barber." And Cohan once admitted that, "as a playwright most of my plays have been presented in two acts for the simple reason that I couldn't think of an idea for a third act."

That statue of the General, and his horse, by the way, ended up across the street from The Plaza. The gilded Civil War memorial is one of the few structures in the area, other than the 1894 Metropolitan Club, older than the hotel.

Years later, Oscar Hammerstein, the musical comedy lyricist and book writer, who teamed up with Richard Rodgers to write some of the greatest musicals in the history of American stagework, was the main force behind erecting a statue of

Cohan on 46th Street and Broadway. It is the only statue of an actor ever erected in Times Square. A region in which, God knows, many an actor has been torn down.

Friends and relatives have always been grateful that celebrated novelist Carson McCullers, who wrote *The Heart Is a Lonely Hunter* and *Reflections in a Golden Eye*, made into a movie with Liz Taylor and Marlon Brando, got to spend her last spring on earth at The Plaza. The chronically ailing but God-fearing McCullers once half-joked that "Sometimes I think God got me mixed up with Job. But Job never cursed God and never have I." But the Columbus, Georgia native, who died in September 1967 at the relatively young age of 50, had suffered a broken leg the spring before she died and she was literally waited on hand and injured foot by The Plaza because she was forced to spend most of her time there in her big Plaza bed and order room service.

Ever the practical joker, novelist John Steinbeck put the power of his fame to test when he tied to get approval for a check for $60 million made out to "cash." Stork Club owner Sherman Billingsly refused to cash it when he spotted the amount but later one unwary Plaza manager unwittingly initialed the check. Needless to say the dumbfounded cashier didn't have quite enough cash on hand.

The Nightclub Era — Hildegarde and the Persian Room

Artists have not just stayed and dined at The Plaza, they've performed there. In addition to being one of the great hotels of the past century, The Plaza has housed one of the era's greatest nightclubs — the legendary Persian Room.

The Great Depression hit The Plaza hard financially, but it was still one of the lucky businesses spared bankruptcy, saved largely by its wealthy, long-term guests (of which the hotel had a large number). Most of these people were independently wealthy widows ("the thirty-nine widows" was how they were described) who never seemed to miss a rent payment or a big tip. Payments, at times, were late from some of those who were not regulars, a Plaza staffer remembered, but the monthly guests never lapsed in their punctuality or their generosity.

The Depression deepened and Prohibition took its toll, but the great Plaza also pulled through the rough financial waters because of its popular tea dances and society banquets. And with the repeal of Prohibition in 1934, manager Henry A. Rost seized on an idea borrowed in part from the success of the tea dances. The Grill was still closed to tea dancing, but the tea court, renamed The Plaza Court, flourished as a gathering place for all ages, where the waiters served dowagers, debutantes and small-fry with equal deference. The Plaza's biggest success during these tough times, however, was its fabled nightclub.

Imagine if you will, a world very much like a Rudolph Valentino movie: exotic and foreign and gaudy in nature, but still with flourishes of regal elegance.

Joseph Urban, an erstwhile scenic designer for the Ziegfeld Follies, was recruited to help transform the Rose Room into the Persian Room. He turned the old Rose Room on the first floor of The Plaza into the glory of old Persia with murals by Lillian Palmedo, and red, red, red everywhere — the draperies, the plush chairs, the carpets of the new Persian Room.

On the night of April 2, 1934, if we could step back in time, we would see professional dancers The De Marcos (who would be lushly accompanied by the Emile Coleman Orchestra), and Tony and Renne. They always performed their set during the spring season (The De Marcos would go all the way to the fall).

Evening dress was "suggested," and a complete dinner from caviar and lobster to strawberries with cream fraiche was $3.

Eddie Duchin, who had lived in the sixth floor suite that was my father's in the 1950's, followed Coleman as bandleader into the room that became what the Rainbow and Stars, the nightclub high atop the RCA (and currently GE) building, always aspired to be.

George Steney would take the Persian Room bandstand with an orchestra as well during the fall of 1934. In 1936, Ray Benson replaced Emile Coleman during the weekdays at the cocktail hour and then in 1937, Velos and Yolanda opened at the Persian Room's spring season with Will McCuen and his Orchestra. He replaced Ray Benson. The team of Velos and Yolanda would come back the following year, this time accompanied by Pancho and his Orchestra at cocktails daily.

Robert Royston, who with his partner Laureen Baldovi were the American Swing Dance Champions from 1995-98, says swing dance exhibitions were as much a part of the early years of The Persian Room as partner dancing came to be in later years.

"The (professional) dancers at the Savoy Ballroom and the Persian Room didn't want to do a dance that everyone could do," Royston, who has been a featured performer in the Broadway musical *Swing*, told me. "Swing dancing was born at Harlem's Savoy Ballroom in 1927 but it wasn't created to be a social dance; it was created to be a competitive dance, a performance dance.

"So at its basic, basic form it's incredibly hard," he said, adding, "The great thing about Jean Velos and some of her colleagues were they were among the first white dancers to do Lindy really, really well, true to its original form, and they brought it to a far more popular level."

"There is no doubt that the Persian Room helped The Plaza out of the financial doldrums," writes Eve Brown. "In its first year, the still depressed 1934, gross receipts of the Room were in the vicinity of twenty-three thousand weekly. It was beginning to look like old times again. A gay if not altogether care-free time."

The ornate Persian Room continued on more or less uneventfully until it was redecorated and refurbished for the 1940 season. It was then that the Dick Gasparro Orchestra came to play. They were well liked, but by the fall of 1941, the Persian Room was looking for something different and new. It would find it on September 23rd at a benefit for the Soldiers and Sailors Club. The songstress would, after that day, be remembered and forever associated with the Persian Room and The Plaza Hotel.

Her name was Hildegarde. and she was an immediate sensation. Her performances gave the Persian Room new life and, after a hiatus in 1942, she would come back in 1943 with a vengeance. In 1944, 1945, 1946. She would not stop. In 1947, after performing all the time, Hildegarde was headlined at the Persian Room when she was joined with three other luminaries in the world of music: Liberace, and Marge and

Gower Champion.

Anna Sosenko, Hildegarde's manager, who helped fashion her client into an international star, says: "The people who came to The Plaza were the great and the near great . . . I felt the room needed a change."

Sosenko and Hildegarde occupied an enormous suite on the so-called "residential" 58th Street side of the hotel, with its own two-elevator bank. As a child visiting my father, I also used these elevators and I recall, from the little I knew of such things, that it had a distinct residential "feel.' Once on the sixth floor, where my father lived, I never thought of it as a hotel but rather a place where people actually lived. Sosenko negotiated a great deal for her suite, which included six months of free rent and half off all food, including room service.

Sosenko told me that at that time she was "all over the place," making sure "everyone who was anyone," was sitting where they should be happy. "I knew who was sitting where and exactly why they were sitting there," she said.

Due to the enormous success of Hildegarde, the Persian Room's seasons became longer and more saturated with famous show performers. Piano aficionado and comedian Victor Borge came on board in September of 1949. In 1950, "Fosse and Niles" appeared at the supper club. The Fosse portion of this teaming was none other than Bob Fosse, who became such a big deal on Broadway.

"I guess I was just born with vitality," Hildegarde mused one time in her Plaza Hotel suite. "It's funny, considering I am anemic and have to have liver injections, but it's just my nature to go out there and work, and I love it."

Anna Sosenko plied her with such admonitions as "get intimate, be natural, be yourself, stand up, show yourself, get out from behind that orchestra, you have a nice figure — why hide it, look up when you sing and look your audience in the face." Sosenko also spent three years in Europe in the Thirties, polishing Hildegarde's act.

Sosenko is one of the reasons Hildegarde believed in fate. Her mother gave her her first piano lessons, spurring her on by promising to wash the dishes while she practiced. She was in Camden, New Jersey staying at the boardinghouse of Anna Sosenko's mother. "And that was fate," Hildegarde once said, "If I hadn't been too poor to stay at the Walt Whitman, I would have never met Anna." The two girls became close friends. When Anna came to New York the following year to try to become a songwriter or newspaperwoman, Hildegarde invited Anna to live in her $12.50 per week apartment on West 89th Street and gave her several dollars a week allowance. "I knew Anna had talent. She had written a great song . . . and she had a certain business acumen I didn't have. We had faith in each other. We stuck together. Thank God we did."

One night dashing Congressman John F. Kennedy was seated at a "ringside" table. He had finished his dinner and was enjoying a song, dessert and an after dinner drink when the great chanteuse suddenly stumbled and almost fell flat on her face. Looking up she said, "You see, Mr. Kennedy, I've fallen for you!"

Singer-director Don Dellair, who toured with Hildegarde before becoming her manager, remembers that, "As a kid growing up in Brooklyn if you wanted to impress your girlfriend you would take her to see Hildegarde because a lot of people couldn't get in. I was going steady one time with this girl and I said, 'I'm taking you out big time,' and when I told her it was Hildegarde the Persian Room she said, 'We'll never get in' and I said, 'Yes, we will,' And when I got to the Persian Room they didn't scare me like they did some of the more well-heeled patrons and finally I made a big stink in the lobby, yelling. 'You're not putting us in there just because we're kids!' And the head waiter came out to shut us up and the other guests said why are you doing this to these kids, 'Let them in!' and we got in.

"Hildegarde broke the barrier of the fourth wall in a supper club," Dellair explains. "She maintained an aura of mystery off stage but never on. She was the one person who made you feel like you were sitting in her living room instead of a supper club."

But Hildegarde's sense of humor often spilled over off stage as well as on. When celebrity photographer Annie Lebowitz was shooting Hildegarde for *Vogue*, she spent hours getting just the right shot. Finally, when Hildegarde sat down at her piano and the pose was just right, Lebowitz, said 'Oh. Hildegarde, that's incredible!' And she turned to Dellair and asked, 'Don, isn't that incredible?!" And Dellair said, "Well actually, she's incomparable!" ' (borrowing the common catch phrase about Hildegarde). And with that, Hildegarde said, 'No, actually, she's uncomfortable!"

It's hard to imagine but Hildegarde became such a sensation (partly because of her phenomenal success selling war bonds) that she had plenty of imitators. Some became renowned in their own right, like Florence Desmond who was booked into The Persian Room herself. On March 9, 1948, they took the stage of The Persian Room together for some songs and fun. "I lovv you everybody becorz I lovv you," Desmond said, imitating Hildegarde.

"Florence Desmond, I don't talk that way!" Hildegarde shot back. Florence was not to be denied: "Oh, yes, becorz, you do!"

Plaza war bond drives during World War II, by the way, raised millions of dollars for U.S. coffers. Ringside seats for what was billed as a "War Bond Fashion Review & Auction with Hildegarde" on June 19, 1944 went for $1000 each. The Plaza opened its rooms as well as its heart and pocketbook to visiting servicemen. Rates for single rooms in 1944 were $10 a night (with an additional 10 cents for each phone call) but some desk clerks took it upon themselves, with their superiors' blessing, to reduce rates for some Army enlisted personnel to a $1 or $2 a night, depending on where they had fought.

※

Big band singer and radio and recording star Margaret Whiting never actually played the Persian Room herself but did the nearby Copacabana on East 60th Street off Fifth Avenue, and many other nightclubs in the 1940s and 1950s and said these venues were much different from the cabaret rooms, like the Oak Room at The Algonquin Hotel and others, today.

"The Persian Room and the St. Regis Roof and others, they were really nightclubs. Cabaret is smaller. And there were big stars who played in them: Steve Lawrence, the Andrews Sisters, so many people became big stars in nightclubs. It was a whole different thing.

"In those days, people would sit in the Persian Room and other lovely rooms and they would have dinner and see a show and then they'd go some other place like the Blue Angel and then they'd go to still some other place for a drink and that was an evening of entertainment. There's really nothing in New York like that anymore."

In 1944, Broadway star Celeste Holm performed at the Persian Room after her triumph as Ado Annie in *Oklahoma!*, the musical that changed the face of American musical history. Kay Thompson, the creator of the fictional Eloise, would then perform the following season, with the Williams Brothers. One of the Williams Brothers was singer Andy Williams, who went on to become a major television and recording star.

In 1950, The Plaza commissioned Henry Dreyfuss, whose firm designed the sleek Art Deco interiors of the famed 20th Century Limited supertrain from New York to Chicago, to modernize Joseph Urban's Art Moderne design. Dreyfuss, to the chagrin of some Plaza regulars, simplified the room dramatically, installing metallic mesh curtains and a white and gold diamond-patterned proscenium.

Nonetheless, Hildegarde, in all her glory, came back and performed in 1958 with the "Diamonds Are A Girls Best Friend" singer, Carol Channing. By December of 1958 the cover charge had gone up to a whopping $3 Monday through Friday and $4 on Saturday.

By the early 1960's, the Persian Room was attracting an

unprecedented number of top names in show business: Abby Lane, Xavier Cugat, Carol Lawrence, Ethel Merman, Kaye Ballard, Leslie Uggams, Juliet Prowse, Dorothy Louden, and the cat-woman herself, Eartha Kitt. Along with Lawrence came Robert Goulet, her husband, in November 1964. He had a brief one-month performance run there. (Note: Hildegarde was not there during this time period.)

Then, it happened. The Vietnam War. It raged on and on during the late 1960's, and the whole nightclub and night time scene in New York became an early casualty. During these turbulent times, the Vietnam War did a lot of damage to this wonderful city, including the death of some of New York's finest newspapers. Many thrived on the nightlife of Manhattan, and died with it.

❋

Cabaret star Andrea Marcovicci remembers her "parents going out in tuxedo and gown, and watching them dance. I went to dancing school . . . So I was one of those New York kids who were just at the tail end of Café Society. And it was really glamour.

"I went to see Abby Lane in the Persian Room. My father and mother took me to see people there. I saw Hildegarde. But I think I saw her at the St. Regis maisonette. I saw everybody when I was a little girl, and they would tease me terribly because they knew all the bandleaders. I'd be about five or six years old and they'd get Emile Coleman and he'd come to the table and he'd say, 'Andrea, would you like to sing tonight?' And he would scare me to death . . . It was all just a joke . . . New York in the 1950's still had some of that glow from the 1930's and 40's just as San Francisco today is what New York was like when I was a girl."

"In the evening you could see the swells in their top hats and tails on opening nights," wrote producer David Brown in *Avenue* magazine. "By dawn, only the street cleaners and dancers and showgirls darting into subways on their way home from work were visible and Broadway looked gray and ashen.

"Walking down Broadway in those years made you feel you were at the center of the earth. The world depression failed to dim its dazzling spectaculars, designed by Douglas Leigh, the 'Lamplighter of Broadway.' His signs were of America — Camels, Chevrolet, Maxwell House Coffee, Pepsodent, Schaeffer Beer, Coca-Cola, and Planter's Peanuts."

※

Late New York City mayor John V. Lindsay, who justly or unjustly got a lot of the blame for caving into union salary demands and helping cause the Big Apple's big 1970s fiscal crisis, made his New York show biz debut with several minutes of onstage patter when he introduced singer Jane Morgan at the Persian Room. In its tongue-and-cheek review of Hizzoner, *Variety*, the show business trade newspaper, called the extraordinarily handsome mayor's curtain raiser in September 1966 "charming," adding that with the plethora of actors becoming politicians "a politico struck back." Henceforth, even after he ran unsuccessfully for President and returned to private law practice, pundits said Lindsay missed his true calling.

※

Some of the final years of the Persian Room were also its best as far as high-profile stars were concerned. Take, for example, fall 1969, through spring 1970:

New York cabaret star Julie Wilson, who would later sing in The Algonquin's Oak Room cabaret in 1984, played The Persian Room several times in the 1960s and 1970s, although she says the experience was "so different" from one decade to the next. The entertainer, who was also in the Broadway Musical *Pajama Game* in the 1950s, recalls that, "The Persian Room was really glamorous and they had John that fantastic maitre'd and he wore tails and he was so elegant."

Wilson has also been a good friend of Hildegarde's over the years.

"I just sent her some roses for her 93rd birthday," Wilson told me when I talked to her after one of her shows at The Algonquin in February 2000. "She called me about two years ago. She said, 'Julie, I saw you sing tonight and I hope you continue as long as you want to. As for me, I've had it. I'm going to bow out. The only thing I might break my word for is if they gave me a lot of money and then my manager would make a lot of money.' Which I thought was so cute."

Although Hildegarde and Sosenko were lovers for years, they never made a public display of their affection. Anna Sosenko died on June 9, 2000 at age 90. After retiring from theatrical management, Sosenko had continued to put on benefits for the Friends of the Theater and Music Collection of the Museum of the City of New York and continued to amass her collection of letters by famous theatrical and literary personalities. She remains best known for helping transform Hildegarde into an international sensation and for composing "Darling, Je Vous Aime Beaucoup," which became Hildegarde's theme song.

"Nobody sang more in the Persian Room than me," said singer, stage and screen star Monique Van Voren. "I was there nine times. One more time was Diane Carroll. Nobody besides her played it more than me."

"It was one of the greatest experiences of my life performing at the Persian Room," said pop singing star and Broadway musical comedy performer Leslie Gore. "I remember working here (in The Plaza's Persian Room) for a solid month. It was a very beautiful room and it was an extraordinary experience. It's one of the more elegant hotels in New York and I think that's why Marty Richards (Broadway producer of *La Cage* and *The Life*) picked it originally for the Red Ball. Remember this is a Valentine's Day and it's about love and the color red and there is something about The Plaza that's just a little bit more special. I was living in New York on 57th Street and I didn't have to stay at The Plaza but very often I came early and had dinner before and I very often took advantage of staying over. It was so much fun. This was probably the early 1970s. I graduated from college in 1968 and so it was probably in 1969 or 1970 that I was here in the Persian Room."

※

Kaye Ballard, appearing at the Persian Room in July 1963, joked that "I've had 20 husbands, five of them my own!"

※

Robert Goulet and actress Carol Lawrence — the latter a star of the then recently opened supersmash *West Side Story* — were married at The Plaza in 1963, a year after Goulet made his nightclub debut at The Plaza's Persian Room. By November 1962, Goulet had spent two years in the cast of the Broadway musical *Camelot* and because of his absolutely striking good looks and deep baritone singing voice had also become somewhat of an international heartthrob. In his Persian Room debut he sang standards of the day like "I'll Get By" and "Life Is Just a Bowl of Cherries" and the Camelot showstopper "If Ever I Should Leave You." Lyn Duddy, who produced Goulet's Persian Room debut said the star's sex appeal came to a fever pitch with his sultry rendition of "Concentrate on One Thing at a Time."

※

"After I came to New York and started playing at The Algonquin Hotel I started learning about the history of cabaret and New York nightclubs. It's largely an oral history, having encountered so many wonderful people like Hildegarde who worked in the clubs. And, again, it's a continuum. It's carrying the torch if you will," said cabaret star and entertainer Michael Feinstein in an interview I had with him in January 2001.

"I wrote Hildegarde a note. And she seems to be doing very well. She's got all of her marbles," Feinstein continued. "I heard her sing in several different events in the last fifteen years. She had extraordinary stage presence. Great charm and impeccable taste in material. She was the first person to record songs from [Gershwin's] *Lady in the Dark*. She was the first person to record Cole Porter songs from *Let's Face It*. She chose a repertoire that was impeccable, was always very imaginative in her appreciation of the songs. She had a wonderful way with the audience. She was very funny and self-deprecating."

Legendary public relations man Lee Solters, who represented The Plaza for several years, says the Persian Room was like Broadway's Palace Theater of the supper clubs. The vaudevillians always wanted to play the Palace Theater. Playing the Persian Room was like a double endorsement. If your manager said you had just played the Persian Room, that was an endorsement. Everyone wanted to play it because that resulted in a boost in salary at other places."

"I remember the Persian Room at its very end," said Donald Smith, New York's cabaret king who organizes the acclaimed cabaret conventions in New York and San Francisco. "And I remember taking Hildegarde to a big party in what used to be the Edwardian Room (now One C.P.S.) in the 1970's and it was very hard to impress Hildegarde. And this hotel manager came over and told us, "We've redone this room to the tune of $2 million.' And Hildegarde, who was sipping her glass of Perrier, turned to him and said, 'You mustn't stint on these things.' "

Then, finally, in 1975, it was all over.

"Persia is out," Donald Trump would say when the time came to revert the Persian Room back to the Rose Room of half a century earlier. "I have a friend who happens to be Iranian, who said, 'Persia is out.' And I said, 'He's right.'"

One-time Persian Room performer Kay Thompson was by this time long officially off The Plaza payroll, but that didn't matter; she had struck her pot of gold in the Fifties. Her book about a little girl who stayed at The Plaza had become an international bestseller. Ms. Thompson didn't have to sing for her supper anymore. She had only to ring for room service and say . . .

"It's Me, Eloise"

I am Eloise
I am six
I am a city child
I live at The Plaza . . .

There is a lobby, which is enormously large with marble
    pillars and ladies in it and a revolving door with
    double-P on it.
I live down at the end of the hall
Sometimes I take two sticks and skidder them along the
    walls
And when I run down the hall I stomp my feel against the
Woodwork which is very good for scuffing and noise
Sometimes I stomp my skates if I want to make a really
    loud
and terrible racket . . .
I am a nuisance in the lobby
Mr. Salomone said so
He is the Manager
I always say "Good morning, Mr. Salomone"
And he always says "Good morning, Eloise" . . .
I live on the top floor

Of course I am apt to be on any floor at any time
And if I want to go anywhere I simply take the elevator
For instance if I happen to be on the second floor I just
Press that button until it comes up and as soon as that
Door is open I get in and say "5th floor please" and
When those doors clank shut we ride up and I get out on
The 5th floor and as soon as that elevator is out of
Sight I skibble up those stairs to the 8th floor and then
I press that button and when that same elevator comes up
    and
As soon as that door is open I get in and say "15th floor
    please."

"Eloise" was born of fatigue. Kay Thompson, one of Hollywood's busiest dancers and choreographers, had arrived late for a Las Vegas engagement. Instead of getting mad at herself for being tardy or yelling and screaming something like "I QUIT! I CAN'T DO THIS ANYMORE," she simply explained to all, "I am Eloise and I am six."

Thompson lived at The Plaza for five years and her "I-am-Eloise-and-I-am-six" impressions became as big a hit with some of the housekeepers and bellboys of the hotel as it did with showbiz people. But the exact origin of Eloise and her voyage from private gag to the printed page has always been a mystery. *Vanity Fair* writer Marie Brenner talked to D. D. Ryan, who as a young fashion editor had introduced Thompson to Hilary Knight, then an obscure illustrator.

Ryan told Brenner: "Kay would call me up and do Eloise on the phone. She would say 'This is Eloise,' in that funny little voice. I finally said, 'There is a fellow . . . a great friend of mine, Hilary Knight.' He used to make little drawings and shove them under my door.

"He lived across the hall. One morning, he made a drawing

of two little girls; one a little, pretty, prissy girl with frizzy blond corkscrews. The other was the complete opposite, and that feisty little girl made me think of Kay's Eloise voice. I told Kay, 'I have a drawing of Eloise' and Kay got enormously interested."

Knight himself wrote in "The Story of Hilary Knight" for the book *Absolutely Essential Eloise*, "The prissy one Kay would call Dorothy Darling. The other suggested the . . . schoolgirls of Ronald Searle. They combined to become the virtual Eloise. Kay Thompson, after our Plaza Hotel meeting, wrote a dazzling outline for Eloise and I began to draw."

A "Christmas card from me to Kay [in 1954] was the first picture of Eloise fully evolved. It led to a year of intense and exhilarating collaboration. And in November, 1955, Eloise was born."

That same year, Kay Thompson published the original *Eloise*, the story of the precocious little rich girl who thought about pouring water down the mail chute, and routinely dialed up a raisin — and seven spoons — from room service.

Brenner got extremely close to interviewing Thompson towards the end of her life, quite a feat considering Thompson wouldn't talk to anyone. "I spent months trying to interview her," Brenner wrote. "She would not allow it, but she did call me on the telephone on several occasions, her voice brimming with enthusiasm. She would not identify herself when she called. She felt there was no need.

"'I do not want my story told. I am too busy working. But do call again. Maybe someday I will talk.' She never did."

I, too, left several messages and notes for Miss Thompson when she lived at 300 East 57th Street, after Liza Minnelli invited her to stay there after Thompson at long last departed The Plaza.

After the original book was published, Kay Thompson's alter ego, Eloise, appeared in baby shops, in department and toy stores, apparel shops and record stores. Best & Company was the New York outlet and Neiman Marcus in Texas.

"Eloise dolls, Eloise dresses were [for] Little Eloises every-where." writes Eve Brown. "In The Plaza there was even an especially decorated Eloise room [closed in 1973] which par-ents brought their children from all over America to see what they had only dreamed about through the wonderful illustra-tions of Hilary Knight. While Thompson repeatedly told every-one the story was patterned after no little girl in particular — besides the figurative little girl inside of her — many people, men as well as women, claimed they were the real Eloise."

In the 1960s a whole new generation of "Eloise" fans was reading the children's book to their children and Thompson, while a devoted follower of the teachings of Christian Science, the followers of which shun alcohol and drugs, found some in the new generation of readers of her book had a different take on an innocent reference to "grass." One young friend of Thompson's, she told an interviewer, referred the author to Eloise talking about her father in this passage in "Eloise:"

> "Here's what he likes
> Martinis;
> Here's what I like
> Grass."

"Do you know she asked me if I meant marijuana," Thompson said. "I told her 'no,' but to read it anyway she wanted to!"

※

"Most people when they speak about the book *Eloise* refer to it as 'Eloise at The Plaza' — and to me it is proof of the insepa-rable connection between the two," Hilary Knight told me.

"Hilary and Kay had a great working relationship when they were working together but later when Kay decided against republishing any but the original *Eloise* book, she became impossible to deal with or talk to," explains Leonard Finger, a prominent TV and film casting agent who is a friend of Knight's.

Adding to the immortality that The Plaza is giving Eloise, The itsy bitsy Entertainment Company, which purchased the rights do movies and a TV series based on the book *Eloise*, is planning to do "Eloise" as an animated children's TV series in 2002.

Kenn Viselman, chairman of itsy bitsy, says "I keep telling people, Eloise may never win a beauty pageant but she is loved by millions and will be adored by many millions more. She's feisty, imaginative and succeeds.

"Steven Spielberg and Tom Hanks' production company and Meg Ryan's production company and Universal and Disney and Warners and everyone wanted *Eloise*," Viselman continued. "I'm this little company that nobody's heard of before and I'm determined that we're going to get this project." And they did, closing the deal with a bravado move on a long L.A. escalator ride.

To celebrate his acquisition of the TV and film rights for *Eloise*, Viselman threw a party at The Plaza in November 1999 which had some of the earmarks of a grand Hollywood movie opening. David Niggli, the chief operating officer of FAO Schwarz, across the street from The Plaza, said, "That evening I kept calling everybody in my office and saying . . . The Plaza is pink! It was spectacular. It was great theater again. Viselman really kind of sweeps you away and you don't see people doing that kind of thing anymore. It was done in the style of *Eloise* and I think when that property was being shopped around, he would've been my first choice to get it, because I think he could understand Eloise. There's a lot of people, particularly in Hollywood, that I was concerned might not understand Eloise because it is a sophisticated property and isn't just for a bratty little girl. There's a lot of adult humor in it that can be adapted for kids that you don't want to lose the aspects because then she's not Eloise anymore. And I think that the kind of event he staged at The Plaza captured it and people walked away knocked out and talking a lot about Eloise."

※

"I know you've heard this before but Eloise was me," one woman wrote The Plaza. And a man, who once worked as a musician at the hotel, insisted he and no one else was the inspiration for the precocious little girl.

To this day, some believe Thompson may have patterned "Eloise" after singer/actress Liza Minnelli, the daughter of Thompson's close friend Judy Garland, who died tragically in 1969 at the age of 46 of a drug overdose.

Adding to the legend that Thompson at least partially drew her inspiration for "Eloise" from Liza Minnelli, who lived with her mother for a time at The Plaza, doorman Joe Szorentini recalls that "Liza used to roller skate up and down 59th Street on the Central Park side with her nanny in the early 1950's."

Liza, by the way, would make her own her own Persian Room debut on February 9, 1965, both defensive and forthright about following in her famous mother's footsteps. "If people want to see my mother in me, I can't help it," she told one interviewer at the time. "People want to see what they want to see. After all, every other girl singer tries to be like her [Judy] just like every man singer tries to be like Frank Sinatra."

Nor was Eloise the first child to turn The Plaza upside down. Some years before, George A. Fuller, Jr., ten-year-old son of the construction company president, drove his custom-built automobile at the scorching speed of twelve miles an hour around the specially built speedway in The Plaza basement. The Plaza basement has seen its fair share of eccentricities, however. Real estate broker Edward Ellsworth resided there at one time in a lavish suite with a specially constructed bath for his French poodle. The poodle also had a personal maid, a personal tutor and room service privileges. (What is it about vast basements that brings out the *Phantom of the Opera* in folks anyway?)

My own personal Eloise theory, which some may find hard to believe, is that writer Kay Thompson may have patterned her little imp after F. Scott Fitzgerald. After all, who flooded his room by letting his bathtub overflow? Who skipped about in the Pulitzer Fountain? Not Eloise. But she poured water down the mail chute, and the outrageous little girl could well have been patterned after the most outrageously talented Jazz Age writer.

But "Kay was adamant that Eloise was her creation," Knight told me. Sybil Goday, the widow of famed record promoter Happy Goday, and one of Thompson's closest friends for nearly forty years, agrees with Knight's assessment. Goday told me that Thompson told her, "Eloise is me," and like she did with so many others, Thompson suddenly broke into her Eloise voice.

"She was Eloise. She always told me that," Goday said.

At least there was no controversy over Eloise's address. Everyone knew she lived at The Plaza. Even those few remaining unenlightened souls learned otherwise when they came across a large oil painting of a saucy six-year-old girl hanging — charmingly if somewhat incongrously amid the other Old World splendor — on a wall of The Plaza's main floor. Hilary Knight had whipped up this masterpiece and for a while it threatened to rival that other New York liberated lady, the Statue of Liberty, as a tourist attraction.

And then one day — the painting disappeared. It had been kid-napped. Probably by a couple of wise-alecks attending a fraternity bash one night at The Plaza (granted, this has never been proved). The Plaza, the city, the world was shocked. Princess Grace of Monoco, was so upset that Knight offered to paint another and donate it to the hotel just to calm her down.

Today, that brand-new portrait (a rather different one, actually) by Hilary Knight hangs from the exact spot the original disappeared.

That makes two mysteries regarding Eloise — her origin and the fate of that first painting. Her creator was also something of an enigma. Thompson's deep religious beliefs, for instance, were not generally known. She was, like stars Ginger

Rogers and Val Kilmer, a Christian Scientist, believing in spiritual healing of physical ills. Often when trying to help friends with problems, from the common cold or various pains, Goday related, Thompson would ask, "Do you have a Bible?" If they said yes, she'd refer them to this or that passage to "uplift" their thoughts. At the same time, Christian Scientists are taught to "honor the child within," the childlike thought that believes that God's goodness can help us right where we are no matter how stubborn the problems.

Kay Thompson died July 6, 1998, while staying in Liza's current apartment at 150 East 69th Street. A Minnelli friend said Liza was in Mexico at the time, and was as broken up about Thompson's death as she had been over Frank Sinatra's the year before.

Eloise had for decades continued to thrive despite Thompson's decision to stop reprinting any but the original Eloise. This was partly because the first TV version of "Eloise," co-starring Mildred Natwick (who would have her greatest success on Broadway in Neil Simon's *Barefoot in the Park* as the ditzy mother-in-law), Monty Woolley, Charles Ruggles, and even Conrad Hilton himself (as himself), was a dud.

Disappointed in the TV movie, and a maverick by her very nature, Thompson stopped the "Eloise" bandwagon in its tracks. She flatly turned down any and all attempts to produce any other film or TV version or reprint subsequent editions of *Eloise at Christmas*, *Eloise in Paris* and *Eloise in Moscow*. Thus, some prices for the original printings of these books soared to $500 a pop.

Nevertheless, "Eloise" had been largely lost to an entire generation. First the painting and then the sequels had simply vanished. In early 1999, after Thompson's death, I asked some colleagues at *People* magazine if "Eloise's" resurgence might be a good idea for a story. A look of bewilderment dropped over their faces. They had never heard of Eloise and didn't realize that a generation earlier "Eloise" had captivated little girls around the country as well as in New York.

Shortly thereafter, Viselman — bringer of The TeleTubbies to the States — obtained the rights from the author's estate for the screen and TV rights for "Eloise" for an undisclosed sum rumored to be in the millions of dollars. The book sequels to the first *Eloise* were also soon rolling off the presses for the first time in decades.

In 1995, for the 40th anniversary of the original publishing, Tom Civitano came up with the idea of the hotel sponsoring an Eloise look-alike contest and the response was overwhelming. All the girl contestants came in for tea. "I love Eloise because she got to live in the hotel and run around and have fun," said the lucky winner.

One family who was peeved at The Plaza even got to have breakfast with "Eloise." "My former boss, who is no longer here with us, promised a lady, who when she came back to The Plaza with her daughter, that she would have breakfast with Eloise," said John Maibach, The Plaza's urbane director of rooms. "He got one of our assistant managers at the front desk and asked our wardrobe manager to go ahead and put together an outfit like Eloise's and his daughter dressed up like Eloise and was having an ice cream sundae under the table, blowing her chocolate milk all over the place, and was running and skipping through the lobby. We created a feeling in a family who will come back time after time."

She is Eloise, but she is really not six. She is timeless.

Balls, Weddings, Potentates, and an Anniversary

L indy hopping was by no means the only hoofing going on at The Plaza. There were still enough lavish parties of all stripes and bangles being held in the ballrooms to make the Astors and the Vanderbilts green in their graves with envy — or start tapping their feet.

The Plaza's annual Red Ball, which has largely succeeded The Waldorf-Astoria's April in Paris Ball as one of the most important annual social events, had another illustrious predecessor. Truman Capote's "Black and White Ball" of 1966.

Capote had been in love with The Plaza ever since he was a copy boy on the *New Yorker* and, for him, it represented what The Waldorf Towers did for Cole Porter — the top. He first frequented The Plaza with friend and fellow novelist Gore Vidal.

In *Capote*, a biography of the temperamental genius, Gerald Clark tells of Capote's Plaza lunches with Gore Vidal. "Gore took Truman to the Everard Baths, a well-known homosexual bathhouse. Truman took Gore to Phil Black's Celebrity Club, a vast, mostly homosexual dance hall in Harlem. Almost every week they met for lunch in the Oak Room of The Plaza, where they nibbled at their friends during the first course, devoured their enemies during the second and savored their own glorious futures over coffee and dessert."

But it wasn't until 1966 that Capote put his own indelible mark on The Plaza in creating The Black and White Ball. The idea came to him in June, and it immediately captured his imagination. He had just received $40,000 for the film rights to his "true fiction" novel *In Cold Blood*. Nothing, he reckoned, could be a better symbol of the new, grown Truman. In one evening he could not only repay all his peacock friends for all their years of entertaining him, but also satisfy a wish he had nursed all his life. Bit by bit, his scheme evolved. The date would be Monday, November 28, 1966; the place, The Plaza Hotel, which, in his opinion, had the only beautiful ballroom left in New York. To add a touch of the fantastic, he settled on a ball masque, like those in storybooks. Inspired by the Ascot scene in *My Fair Lady*, which Cecil (Beaton) had costumed in black and white, he decided to call his party the Black and White Ball and require his guests — the characters in his own play — to dress in nothing else.

In a master stroke of social manipulation, Capote made Washington *Post* publisher Katharine Graham the guest of honor, hoping that her intellectual and social standing would add weight to what was soon to become "the" social event of the year.

Hand-addressed invitations read:

> *IN HONOR OF MRS. KATHARINE GRAHAM*
> *MR. TRUMAN CAPOTE*
> *REQUESTS THE PLEASURE OF YOUR COMPANY*
> *AT A BLACK AND WHITE DANCE*
> *ON MONDAY, THE TWENTY-EIGHTH OF NOVEMBER*
> *AT TEN O'CLOCK*
> *GRAND ROOM, THE PLAZA*

But as 10 P.M. came and went some organizers exchanged worried glances: only a handful of revelers had assembled in the Grand Ballroom. But at 10:30, in a driving rain, masked guests began to queue up in limousines. Capote and Graham were among the early arrivals, dressed as "The Maharajah and Maharani of Jaipur."

After spending a large fortune on the ball itself, Capote repeatedly bragged his mask cost a mere 39 cents. Clark, in his book, reports that the costumes of famous guests were both elaborate and oddball: "Candice Bergen's mask was topped by giant rabbit ears. . . . Frank Sinatra's had cat whiskers. Mrs. John Converse, Gary Cooper's widow, wore black velvet, from which sprouted a gardenia tree bearing live blooms."

Capote told one interviewer that he "decided that everyone invited to come stag had to be either very rich, very talented, or very beautiful, and of course preferably all three." Graham recalled in her autobiography *Katharine Graham: Personal History* that "Truman had planned everything, down to the last detail . . . He and I went to the Paleys' [William Paley, CBS chairman, and his wife, Babe] for a drink and then left for The Plaza. We had to go through a crowd that was gathering in front . . . almost 200 television and still cameras in the lobby . . . I had never seen anything like it."

The first annual Red Ball was held at The Plaza in February, 1995, and it, like succeeding Red Balls, helped raise money for two charities inspired by the recently deceased Mary Lea Johnson, daughter of Seward Johnson, Jr., son of one of the Johnson & Johnson's. The two charities were the Mary Lea Johnson Richards Institute at New York University Medical Center and the Children's Advocacy Center in Manhattan. Mary Lea had been the recipient of a liver transplant and wanted others who needed one to be able to get it at the Institute. Likewise, Mary Lea had reportedly been abused when she was a child, and her Advocacy Center assists those similarly victimized.

Over the years, the Red Balls have attracted countless celebrities much the same as Capote's Black and White Ball did. Singers Michael Bolton and Naomi Judd were honored at the 1999 Red Ball which included many VIP's of stage, screen and society.

But The Plaza's Grand Ballroom has played a role in charity and war relief events almost from the moment it opened in 1907. Socialites dined and danced for the "Bundles for Britain" ball during World War II and American servicemen were invited to weekly dances in the ballroom. Mrs. Charles C. Auchincloss and other society matrons held tea dances for American officers in The Plaza's Grill Room, later renamed the Edwardian Room — and later still, One C.P.S.

The Plaza won prizes for its war bond drives but topped itself and every other hotel in the city when its sixth bond drive sold $1.4 million for the war effort. Other Plaza patrons opened their hearts as well as their pocketbooks to American servicemen footloose in New York. Mrs. Charles O. Maas, whose late husband had been President Roosevelt's Naval Aide, threw a series of parties for servicemen, including a Washington's Birthday bash for 300 troops in the Grand Ballroom in 1942. She also hosted half a dozen servicemen for Sunday night super in her suite. And on V-J Day (Victory over Japan) on August 14, 1945, when it seems that the celebrations from Times Square itself had flooded the lobby and halls of the hotel, there was the elderly Mrs. Maas was, at least for a short while, whooping it up with the delirious troops dancing in the hotel's marble halls. A full year after World War II ended, the Persian Room pitched in with other New York nightclubs like the Latin Quater and Leon & Eddie's to raise money for a very worthy cause called the War Wounded Christmas Fund to make it possible for those who had been incapacitated in the war and were in New York area hospitals to make telephone calls home for the holidays.

The first International Debutante Ball was held at The Plaza in 1954. It introduced some of the daughters of Ambassadors to the United States and United Nations, as well as those of well-to-do American families around the country, to society.

But perhaps the oddest black-tie event occurred in the carefree, Roaring Twenties, when a prize fight was staged in the glittering Grand Ballroom for the benefit of the New York *American* (newspaper) Christmas Fund. Organized by society honcho A. J. Drezel Biddle, Sr., an amateur boxer himself, the charity match drew the likes of Mrs. Reginald C. Vanderbilt, Mrs. George Washington Kavanaugh, Corbina Wright, and a plethora of Belmonts, Rhinelanders and Chryslers, who, once the bout was in full swing, sounded more like roustabouts in the upper tiers of Madison Square Garden than the gentry of Fifth and Park Avenues.

The Plaza is also justly renowned for its weddings. It's a full service hotel, after all. After it introduces all those debutantes, it no doubt feels a certain obligation to see them properly wed some months later. Although not everyone who gets hitched at The Plaza is a debutante.

Donald Trump's words, "of course, the money was unlimited" still echo in my thoughts. The Eddie Murphy wedding in March 1993 was one of the most beautiful and perhaps costliest ever at The Plaza. Everything had been adorned in white, including a new white rug that had been laid in the Grand Ballroom just for the occasion. The chairs had been covered in white satin, as had the ceiling, providing an Arabian tent-like effect that completely masked the gilded ballroom.

The bride, Nicole, and the groom, star of *Beverly Hills Cop* and other blockbusters, spent their wedding night in the 7,802-square-foot Presidential Suite with its panoramic view of Central Park. They would find that their suite — really a small house on the 17th floor — had five bedrooms and that they could venture out to a big terrace for a cocktail served by the suite's very own maid. The usual cost for the suite is $15,000, but in Murphy's case it was included in the overall price of the wedding.

Nicole and Eddie's pre-wedding hideaway, the 2,818-

square foot Vanderbilt Suite (533-543), was far from shabby either. Overlooking the Fifth Avenue side of the hotel, it boasts three bedrooms and a Jacuzzi. And like the Presidential Suite, its $3,000 a night price tag had been waived as part of the wedding. It was here that Nicole and her bridesmaids could spread out to get dressed for the rehearsal dinner and wedding parties.

On hand to celebrate the occasion were Wayne Newton, Quincy Jones, Nastassia Kinski, Bill Murray and Bruce Willis, among many other celebrity buddies.

The actual wedding ceremony was held in The Plaza's Grand Ballroom; there was a sit-down dinner for five hundred in the Terrace Room and by the time that was over, the Grand Ballroom had been converted into a disco. The beat went on almost until dawn.

Unlike the Trump wedding discussed earlier, the preparations for the Eddie Murphy wedding started months before the actual date. What in the lingo of hotels is called the "set-up" didn't come until several days before the wedding.

"We started on Thursday for a Sunday wedding," Paul Nicaj, former Plaza Director of Banquets and Restaurants and currently at The Pierre, explains. "We had a Friday evening dinner. After dinner, we started the Murphy set-up."

At the same time, there were several functions in between the start of the set-up and the actual wedding.

"We had a St. Patrick's Day function in the Grand Ballroom But they didn't mind it. They actually loved what we had done already. We already had the chiffon up in the ceiling and the lights were up, so the major hard part of the set-up was already done before the day of the wedding."

One of the nicest things about a wedding, Nicaj says, is that "people bring their kids and show them where they got married, and they still remember me — and that's the biggest reward. There are no other rewards."

Like an actor, Nicaj and his crew can't afford to let down while they're "on." "You must give the perfect service at the sixteenth hour as you do in the first hours, to smile as you did the first three hours. Not to lose it, and it's hard to do that, but you've got to remember you're always on stage when you're in front of people. And it's a tough challenge because you can't aggravate people in the back of the house (kitchens, etc.), because if you anger them, they'll show their anger back to the guest inside, so it's a total challenge in performance. I am very demanding when it comes to service, but fair and firm. That's my management style."

Lawrence Harvey, the executive director of catering at The Plaza, in his book, *Plaza Weddings*, points out some of the differences between how weddings were planned years ago and how they're done today.

"Once, the mother would make all the arrangements," he writes. "The father would come in for the financial part. Now many times it's the bride who comes in and sets up her own wedding. Often, I don't even meet the parents until much later."

Harvey also talks about personalizing weddings to weave in a family story and has many tips about starting a wedding off to make everyone feel more at ease.

When Joan Rivers' daughter, Melissa Rivers, got married at The Plaza, Harvey says Rivers had the Gay Men's Choir serenade the guests as they entered through the Palm Court and walked up the stairs to the Terrace Room. And when Joan Rivers entered the Terrace Room, the choir broke out into a rousing rendition of "Hey, Big Spender!"

Joan and Melissa Rivers, who had lived on Fifth Avenue overlooking Central Park for years, also wanted to incorporate some of the feeling of the park in Melissa's wedding so they used 20-foot high white birch trees, white carpeting and white chairs in the Terrace Room to give it the feeling of a midwinter snowy day in Central Park.

In 1994, The Plaza launched a wedding and honeymoon promotion that was unparalleled even for marketing-savvy New York hotels. The hotel wanted to have honeymooners who stayed at the hotel 25 years ago or more to come back and pay the same rate they did originally. "The problem for us was that we had no guest history that far back," said Tom Civitano, the hotel's longtime vice president of sales and marketing. "So we decided that in order to qualify they must have their original hotel bill. I was amazed at how many people kept their hotel bill from their honeymoon at The Plaza."

Like the Eddie Murphy wedding, the Michael Douglas-Catherine Zeta-Jones wedding of November 18, 2000 was an affair of the heart that would give any average person's bank account a coronary.

Indeed, the guest list was fit for the Queen of England, let alone the Hollywood elite. Aside from nearly a hundred family and close personal friends, the invited included such A-list goers as UN Secretary General Kofi Annan, Goldie Hawn, Meg Ryan and new (albeit not for long) beau Russell Crow.

"It was Gregory Peck marrying Audrey Hepburn," filmmaker and guest Oliver Stone (who'd directed Douglas in *Wall Street*) told *People* magazine.

The night before the nuptials, Michael and Catherine came to a food tasting in the kitchen of The Plaza prepared by executive chef Bruno Tison. To Bruno's great surprise, "they were very, very knowledgeable about food. You know, I was quite nervous at first because of Michael Douglas — he plays all those tough guys roles. But he was quite nice. It turned out that they were both so down to earth people. Knowledgeable about food. We cooked everything from appetizers to main courses to desserts. One of each. And they had trouble making a decision. They tasted every dish. They complimented every dish. You could see they knew about food. They brought a party planner. The party planner had nothing to say. They were hesitating for the main course between a venison and a rack of lamb and the party planner suggested to put the garnishes and the vegetables from the venison with the rack of lamb. And Catherine Zeta-Jones said, 'The vegetables and the sauce from the venison don't go with the rack of lamb. It's two different tastes!'

"And it's true. They're two different tastes. Venison goes more with sweet and sour vegetables."

Hello magazine got a chance to speak to the happy couple, pre-nuptials, and asked them how, since they had the resources to get married any place on the globe, they had ended up in midtown Manhattan.

"We looked in a couple of places in Majorca and we thought about a couple in Wales," Michael Douglas answered. "And we did some initial design plans for my hotel in Bermuda, Aeriel Sands, but it's a little dicey in Bermuda this time of year, weather-wise, and Majorca is a long distance for all of our friends from California to come, so it just became, well, why not just right here in New York? You can get everything here."

His bride added, "Also it's a wonderful time in New York and every time we walk down the street, people in vans scream at Michael: 'Hi! Glad you're back!' So we feel welcome here. Also, The Plaza Hotel, for me, means New York. There are so many beautiful, modern hotels that have sprung up, but there's just something about The Plaza. A lot of my friends and family have never even been to New York before, so they are so excited about staying there."

※

Over the years, The Plaza has had a lot of parties and even weddings for members of some of New York's crime families. But nothing quite as wild as when one "family" member demanded that he pay the bill in cash and may have gotten inadvertently hustled in the process.

"They did a lot of business with us at The Plaza. They always paid right away," Philip Hughes said. "One time a member of the family had a wedding and they paid me that day, they didn't wait for a bill, in cash. They didn't want to write a check. And I didn't know the exact cost of the wedding and I just had to kind of wing it. I winged it on the high side just to cover myself! And they paid me cash out of a traveling case.

They opened it up and counted it out."

❋

There are many varieties of fetes held at the hotel, however. While doing my interviews in the second floor banquet department, the staff was anticipating a visit by Liza Minnelli. She was planning to have a 50th birthday party at The Plaza. "My cousin worked with Liza in *Cabaret*," Bobby D'Angelo commented. "He was a professional dancer since he was five years old. Liza. I can't believe she's 50. ("Liza's the ultimate survivor," Minnelli friend Stewart F. Lane, who co-produced *Minnelli on Minnelli*, told me. "She's learned from her mother's mistakes and she's willing to be helped by friends")

❋

The Plaza often entertains a United Nations clientele among its paying guests.

Martin Riskin, who went on to become an executive at The Waldorf, started his career in the banquet department of The Plaza. "I trained there after my U.S. Army service in the 1960s," Riskin says. "Our banquet department was a little United Nations. The executives consisted of one man who was Swiss, two were German, one was Hungarian, and one was Czech. I was the only American. Our executive chef was French. The banquet headwaiter was Greek, and my secretary was from Latvia. If this wasn't a United Nations! And everyone got along so beautifully. We had great pride in The Plaza. It was a very international staff."

Riskin was privy to many diplomatic tales at The Plaza, including one that involved the President of Finland. The president, Riskin said, felt very nervous because our Secretary of State was coming to Finland and as he said, "We Finns don't speak English and we don't know what to do in the United States." He was told, "The big American plane will fly into Helsinki and we will have the red carpet out, television cameras and all of the photographers and the brass band. So when

Secretary of State Kissinger comes down from the plane, say 'Welcome to Finland, Mr. Kissinger.' And then he will talk for half an hour. Then when you get into the limousine just smile and say, 'How are you?' So Mr. Kissinger got out of the plane and everything went as scheduled.

"Kissinger had talked for half an hour, maybe more, and then they got into the limousine and started to go to Helsinki, whereupon the president of Finland smiled and in his broken English said, 'Who are you?'"

Foreign dignitaries do sometimes have to "spread out," book entire floors, and even try to change the hotel's existing room configuration if they can to suit their own individual entourage.

The King of Morocco, His Majesty King Hassan II, the son of Mohammed V, rented three entire floors for three months on one unusually long stay in 1984 around the time he formally addressed the General Assembly of the United Nations. He wanted to connect all the rooms on all three floors at his own expense. The hotel turned him down but Philip Hughes, the hotel's general manager at the time, heartily accepted the King's down payment — a leather suitcase containing half a million cash.

Two decades earlier, King Hassan II of Morocco did things on a grand scale outside the hotel. On a single shopping spree he practically bought out one department store and made a serious dent in the showrooms of Ford and Cadillac dealerships in Manhattan. This occasion was in 1963, according to Plaza records. The King had talked to the delegates of fifty-five nations. He and his family were on the 14th floor. The head of the Ministry of Public Works was on the 13th floor, the Director of Handicrafts and Director of Tourism had come along for what was a major trade mission.

At a Cadillac showroom, a lady sales clerk asked the king, "Five Cadillacs, Your Majesty?" And he answered, "Uh-huh. Yes, five."

During a number of his visits to America and to The Plaza,

the king received the "royal treatment" from the U.S. State Department; that is, the top U.S. State Department officials checked into quarters near the King. For example, on February 17, 1967, the King of Morocco's party took most of the 14th floor and a room on the 13th. His Majesty Hassan occupied Room 1401, 1405, 1407, and 1411, which are on the Central Park South side of The Plaza facing the park and connected to each other by inner doors. His Majesty's brother, Prince Muoulay Abdallah, was in Suite 1427, 1429 and 1431. Her Royal Highness, Princess Lalla Nezha, and his Majesty's sister, occupied Suites 1417, 1419, and 1421.

At the same time, the Honorable Angier Biddle Duke, Chief of Protocol of the United Nations, and his wife were in Suite 1301-5, the floor just below the King's. George J. Szabo, a USA Information Agency photographer, got Room 1454.

Besides being attended by official escorts from the United States, representatives of The Plaza also took special care to greet top foreign dignitaries like the King of Morocco. On the king's visit to New York and The Plaza in 1991, for example, owner Donald Trump personally greeted him.

The previous fall, when the king had arrived for the U.N. General Assembly, Trump reported to various members of the media that "We are honored to have some twenty-eight delegations staying at The Plaza" for the U.N. General Assembly.

Publicist Eve Brown was working at The Plaza when Hassan II stayed at the hotel in the 1960s:

"The smell of burning incense was everywhere on The Plaza's fourteenth floor when Hassan II of Morocco was in residence for ten days in April 1963. Like the Russians, the Moroccans had brought their own cooks — but unlike the Russians they did not cook in their rooms.

"Because of their religious beliefs and taboos of certain foods, the handling of meals for the Muslims was left entirely to them. In respect for their native customs, The Plaza turned over a large section of its kitchens to the Moroccan cooks. Plaza chefs had no part of the food arrangements, but the steward would find out beforehand what was required for the meals served the party in their rooms and purchase it.

"A memorandum to The Plaza food and beverage staff, just before the arrival of the king and his entourage, directed that the 'entire catering department, especially Room Service, must be ready to give special service.' Dates, figs, goats' milk, goat cheese and mint tea were especially ordered for them. Since alcoholic beverages are denied Muslims, they consumed gallons of orange juice, soft drinks and coffee, and pounds of bonbons and other candies to satisfy the well-known Moroccan sweet tooth. Pork and beef were taboo, but chicken and lamb permitted. Many a Plaza kitchen helper learned the method of roasting a whole lamb. Five whole roasted baby lambs graced the buffet at a party for the king in the ballroom."

Ethiopian Emperor Haile Selassie also stayed at The Plaza when he attended a conference at the United Nations. His granddaughter, the apple of his eye, Princess Ruth, accompanied the conquering Lion of Judah. In the absence of his royal lions, he proved to be a wonderfully gentle little man, with smiling eyes and exquisite politeness, plus a healthy appetite. "His visit caused no food crises at The Plaza," Brown wrote. "As a Coptic, he had no food prohibitions; a preference for high-protein foods probably was the secret of his slimness and energy.

"Despite his age, the Emperor had tremendous stamina. At a reception in his honor in the Grand Ballroom, he stood in the receiving line for hours, shaking hands and acknowledging the bows of something like a thousand guests. If it taxed the energy of this elderly man, he never showed it."

While Hassan's visits were always challenging to The Plaza kitchen, Premier Nikita Khrushechev of the former Soviet Union proved to be equally daunting to Plaza security.

"When Khrushechev reached the elevators, he expressed annoyance that a car was not waiting to whisk him to the reception. Here a sizable group of people reacted with disapproval," writes Eve Brown. "Khrushchev turned quickly and stuck out his tongue at them. Security forces literally took over the lobby. Happily, no more untoward incidents occurred."

Along with the American flag, four foreign flags are displayed on the five flagpoles flying from the balcony of the Fifth Avenue entrance of the hotel, but when Khrushchev was to arrive late one afternoon in 1960 the flags, all five of them, had been lowered to be put away for the evening. Quick-thinking manager Neal Lang ordered both the Stars and Stripes and the Soviet Hammer and Sickle hung in a hurry and the Soviet premier proudly entered the hotel under his country's red flag.

❈

Haughty fashion models and world dictators. Hotel guests don't come any more demanding than that. The Plaza strives to please, regardless. But not all of The Plaza's spectacular bashes are for strangers. They occasionally throw a lavish occasion for themselves.

The Plaza's 60th anniversary in 1967 was without a lot of the fanfare of the 50th but accolades poured in nevertheless. *Esquire* magazine travel editor Richard Joseph simply rated The Plaza the greatest hotel in the world, ahead of his second-placed Gritti Palace in Venice and third-ranked Mauna Kea Hotel in Hawaii, the brainchild of Laurance Rockefeller.

Joseph explained at the time that "The Plaza remains and island of continental elegance" and has "maintained its opulence and elegance . . . and kept up its rare standard of service."

On October 1, 1982, The Plaza celebrated its diamond anniversary; the grand hotel was officially three quarters of a century old. That day, *The New York Times* duly reported (in a somewhat unecstatic prose) that "the fall social season finally exploded with parties and receptions, private and public, large and small."

At The Plaza, Brooke Astor, Alice Kaplan, and 378 of New York's social, political and business men and women "wined and dined the night away in the hotel's resplendent grand ballroom and its Terrace Room, adjoining the Palm Court."

A Rolls Royce Silver Ghost was dutifully parked outside the Fifth Avenue entrance between the hotel and the Pulitzer Fountain. There two yeomen of the guard trumpeted the arrival of the resplendent guests. Down the red carpet leading to the front door strolled Estee Lauder, John Loeb, and society bandleader Peter Duchin. The red carpet continued on straight through from the Palm Court to the Terrace Room. In the ornate Terrace Room and Grand Ballroom, the guests who'd already been announced were swinging and swaying to turn-of-the-century music, played by the other members of The Peter Duchin Orchestra.

The $500-a-plate 75th anniversary gala benefited the New York Landmarks Conservancy, the nonprofit group founded in 1972 to protect New York City buildings of particular historical or architectural interest. Then New York City Mayor Ed Koch stopped by briefly to give his best wishes to The Plaza and the Landmarks Conservancy. Most of the other guests danced until well past midnight. (At The Plaza, where some members of society greet each other with words along the lines of "I'm 873 Park Avenue, who are you?" the night was still young even if the hotel no longer was.)

For Duchin, playing seemed like another homecoming. Not because he plays there regularly, which he certainly does, but because he was there when his father, the late bandleader Eddie Duchin and his society-born mother, lived in suite 658-660. This I know from my reservoir of personal experiences, since my father and stepmother lived in that same suite eleven years after the Duchins.

Otto Schmidt, who was the general manager of the Peter Duchin Orchestra during the time of The Plaza Hotel's 75th Anniversary, also had formerly been part of the orchestra for many years at the Persian Room. At the gala anniversary event, Schmidt and The Plaza's special events people positioned eight musicians on the side landing of the Terrace Room — the reception area for the VIP's going to the main event inside the Grand Ballroom. The band members were all dressed in formal attire. Ten more members were placed on the small rise on the stage. The cost of the orchestra in 1982 was $5,200 for the evening — not bad considering it was the most publicized party at The Plaza since Truman Capote's Black and White Ball.

Also on hand were the Tintypes, a five-singer group and piano accompanist. They were dressed in turn-of-the-(nineteenth)-century formal wear and performed such hits of the time as "I Don't Care" and "In Old New York."

"There are glitzier, snootier and more exclusive hotels in New York," Beth Fallon wrote in her column in the New York *Daily News* in October 1982. "None is a patch on The Plaza, where glitz, snootiness and ineptness masquerading as exclusivity are held in low esteem."

Fallon went on to tell one reason she held The Plaza in her high esteem when, asked to be a bridesmaid in a big formal New York wedding, a bellboy at the hotel carried her outfit a block in a snowstorm and then refused to take a tip.

As part of its 75th anniversary, The Plaza held a two-week festival in mid-September at Cinema 3, the intimate movie theater in the hotel's lower level near Trader Vic's. Among the films featured were *North by Northwest*, *The Great Gatsby*, *The Rose*, and *Breakfast at Tiffany's*, all partly shot in or around the hotel.

The Plaza is a repository of millions of different memories, much like a bank with money. Except that, with memories, almost everyone who cares to share does. For The Plaza is a place "where private elegance meets public grandeur and both come off the better for it," according to the Paul Goldberger.

"The Plaza is truly a way of life. There's no hotel in New York that that can be said of. There will always be a newer hotel and grander hotel . . . but The Plaza has stayed the course," says Clint Wade, a top New York public relations man, who represented The Plaza for some years, most notably for its 75th anniversary celebration.

"For everyone we had a different function," Wade elaborates

on that jubilee year, "which culminated in the actual grand ball on October First. I must say it was one of the most exciting times in my life. Brendan Gill and I worked together closely. We hit every aspect of what made The Plaza important to New York and New York important to The Plaza; what The Plaza meant to children; what The Plaza meant to architecture. And the Shinn paintings. The social landmark."

The late, legendary, travel writer Horace Sutton, who had attended more than his share of splendid anniversary parties, said it was one of the best series of anniversary celebrations of any in his long memory. Tins of caviar were imported from Russia, lobsters from Maine. Black angus steak. Superlative sauces of every hue and texture and taste.

The Plaza continued celebrating its 75th anniversary with a menu in the Edwardian Room highlighting the culinary triumphs of five of The Plaza's world renowned chefs. Selections from past master chefs Eugene Laperruque, Pierre LaFarge, Leopold Lattard, Humberto Gatti, and Joseph Trombetti, were offered.

Here's the bill of fare — so you can at least eat your heart out:

"[In] honor of the occasion there will be a specially created Edwardian Room Anniversary Dinner for $34," the hotel management announced. "This will include a selection of appetizers followed by a choice of entrees: Tournedo Belle Helene (a tenderloin with truffles and asparagus croquette); Supreme of Chapon Plaza (a breast of capon on toast with a brandy cream sauce — created by Chef Humberto Gatti); Poisson Grille Maitre d'Hotel (broiled tile fish with herbed butter). Brie, port Salute or dessert from the trolley will then be offered. The dinner will also include a bottle of Plaza Label Mumm's Cordon Vert Champagne.

"A sampling of the other entrees for the celebration will include: Gigot d'Agneau LaFarge (leg of lamb with mint sauce — first created by Chef Pierre LaFarge of The Plaza); Saumon en Croute au Beuree Blanc (mousse of salmon in golden crust);

and Homard Thermidor (stuffed lobster, simmered with cream, mushrooms, spices and a touch of brandy).

"A featured item will be The Plaza 75-cent cocktail, which is made up of The Plaza's Private Label Champagne and a splash of Chambord. The champagne is G.H. Mumm Cordon Vert which Browne Vinters has bottled expressively for The Plaza.

"To add to this tribute to fine dining, the Edwardian Room will have new lace overlays on pink tablecloths, as well as new glasses and table accessories designed especially for the occasion.

"In keeping with popular custom, music will be provided nightly by Roger Stanley and dancing Tuesday through Sunday nights from 6 P.M. to 12:30 A.M."

※

There was one infamous occasion, of course, when the legendary Plaza service broke down utterly. It was February 1969. Feminism was at its height, and NOW came to dine in architect Henry Hardenbergh's favorite room, the Men's Grill, which heretofore had strictly adhered to its name, its seating policy every bit as chauvinistically late Victorian as the room furnishings. When Betty Friedan, president of the National Organization for Women arrived in the grill at high noon with a few female would-be-dining companions, they took a center table and waited and waited to be served. Every waiter passed them by, except to come by at one point and pointedly remove the table from the ladies' midst.

"It seems as if we're not going to be served," announced Friedan to her company, which included Diana Gartner, NOW's vice-president. That day, the battle went to tradition, but within the year, the Men's Grill (as well as the even gruffer McSorley's Old Ale House, an all-male bar for 117 years downtown in the East Village), had finally opened their doors to "the opposite sex." One might even say it was the end of an ERA.

Nor has everyone relished the superb haute cuisine served up by The Plaza. For Frank Lloyd Wright, who lived at The

Plaza during those years his Guggenheim Museum was being constructed farther up the avenue, the food was about the only thing he disliked about the place. Because he was sick of the rich food he was always served, his sister, Maginol Wright Barney, had to ferry baked potatoes up to him in a brown paper bag. To be fair to The Plaza's chefs, Wright followed this austere custom not only at The Plaza but at lunches and dinners around town.

Ever the perfectionist, hotel sources say the extremely orderly Wright demanded that any leaks in facets or burnt out light be fixed and replaced immediately. But, apparently, he was not as fastidious about imperfections associated with his own work. My family was given a three-acre island in the Thousand Islands in Canada by Irene Purcell, a Broadway actress who had married a Johnson Wax heir and didn't want the island any more. The Johnsons owned the fabulous Wright-designed "Wingspread" mansion in Wisconsin and the story goes that Johnson ran to the phone to call Wright during a dinner party when rain was leaking in through the roof. "Think nothing of it," Wright supposedly told Johnson on the phone. "But the rain is falling into the lady guest of honor's soup plate!" Johnson cried. "Tell her to move her chair," Wright shot back.

After Frank Lloyd Wright died his widow Oligivanna Wright and their daughter Iovanna used to stay at The Plaza in what had been Wright's old third floor suite overlooking Central Park whenever they were in New York.

The kind of food that offended Frank Lloyd Wright was the very kind that Lucius Beebe, the man-about-town, writer and hotel connoisseur extraordinaire, wrote about in the April 1949 *Holiday* magazine, an issue entirely devoted to New York City: "Today there are still standing two superplush examples of hotel style of the 1900's; The Plaza and St. Regis, which boast among their resources liveried footmen, solid gold dinner services, fabulous champagne bins and menus studded with pheasant Souvaroff and peaches flambees; whose regular patrons take single eyeglasses, Rolls-Royces and the oldest titles of Europe as the merest commonplaces."

During these early years of the last century extravagance certainly still reigned supreme at The Plaza. At one party during winter 1930, the Grand Ballroom was transformed into southern gardens; at another, in summer, it became a Swiss hideaway. Some of these parties cost $100,000, a fantastic sum for those days, and still not chopped liver these days. The Plaza's gain was the Waldorf's loss and vice-versa, as there remains, over the years, a healthy sense of competition between the two hotels.

Location had helped to kill the old Waldorf, left almost marooned, an ancient island of luxury from the previous century. It was below 42nd Street, which at one time had been the only place fashionable society wanted to be, but eventually became where department and electronics stores and fast-food restaurants wanted to be.

The Plaza has throughout its nearly one hundred years weathered such trends largely by being blessed with superb ambassadors for managers. Manager Phil Hughes once said no to the King of Morocco's request that he be allowed two floors of the hotel, while Plaza manager Richard Wilhelm found he didn't have to cater to the demands of all his star clientele, especially if they wanted the same suite on the same night.

Singer LaToya Jackson, for example, had been accustomed to the $3,000 a night Vanderbilt Suite, the second largest specialty suite in the hotel. But it had already been promised to a committee of the Vice President, Dan Quayle.

"Anyway," Wilhelm said, "the Vice President ended up having it because it was already set up for security."

In the polished way that many hoteliers have, Wilhelm told Jackson's agent he very much wanted to live up to the commitment to give Ms. Jackson the Vanderbilt Suite, so he'd provide another suite called the Astor. He stressed it had "a very large boudoir. We took three guestrooms and made it into one large boudoir — on the park."

While her agent remained unconvinced, Ms. Jackson ended up falling in love with the Hollywood style boudoir — with the bathtub overlooking Central Park.

And why would The Plaza turn three guest rooms — maybe it was only two — into a bathroom, regardless of the view? Well, the hotel could get possibly $400 to $450 a night for a single room on the park. Make two or even three rooms into one big one and you can charge $3000 a night for the bathroom and an adjoining bedroom. It's that simple. It's also how a great hotel skirts bad financial times — by catering to its core rich clientele. It's a recession strategy most of us are not entitled to.

The Astor boudoir, by the way, has three parts to it. There is the lady's portion, the gentleman's portion with a steam shower, and then right in the middle facing the park is a large Jacuzzi raised up on a marble pedestal.

"Right there is your bubble bath," said Wilhelm, "with a glass of crystal champagne, overlooking Central Park."

I couldn't actually picture myself doing this — I'd worry too much about all of Central Park overlooking me. But perhaps that's why I'm neither rich nor famous.

※

Not all Plaza events are fun and games. In a major break with the Communist Party of the Soviet Union, Stalin's daughter, Svetlana Alliluyeva, held a televised news conference at The Plaza on April 26, 1967, telling the world the responsibility of the killings under her father's brutal regime should be shared by Communist officials. "They should not accuse one person of the crimes in which so many people were involved."

Perhaps the most dramatic thing to happen at The Plaza in its long history wasn't the invasion of The Beatles but the near assassination in April 1970 of National Chinese Vice Premier Chiang Ching-Kuo, the son of Chiang Kai-Shek. Ching-Kuo was coming through a revolving glass door on the Central Park South entrance of the hotel when New York City Police

Department Detective Henry Suarez knocked a 25-caliber gun out of the hand of Peter Huang, a member of a group picketing the Vice Premier's visit outside The Plaza, but not before a bullet from the gun hit the glass in the door. Ching-Kuo, momentarily shaken, went upstairs to talk to a group of business and political leaders gathered in the Grand Ballroom and had the presence of mind not to even mention the incident.

When members of fifty-one nations descended on New York on October 21, 1946, for the first historic meeting of the UN General Assembly, The Plaza played an important role in housing some of the Soviet delegation, Byelo-Russian and Ukranian delegations which were scattered among The Plaza and several other hotels. The visit was also a major test of whether New York would be chosen for the world headquarters of the UN which it was.

King Hassan II of Morocco left The Plaza on February 10, 1967, with a retinue of 130 on his way to the White House where he received an historic pledge from President Lyndon Johnson of $15 million in arms to bolster Morocco's defenses.

Like many great institutions, The Plaza, its staff as well as its guests, often caters to those on the opposite ends of the great American political spectrum indiscriminately. However, rarely do they change their political leanings as much as Roger Sonnabend, president of The Hotel Corporation of America, which owed The Plaza in the 1960s between the Hilton and Trump regimes. Sonnabend, who was Jewish, attended Phillips Exeter Academy prep school and the Harvard Business School, was a confirmed Republican until he became appalled with his own laissez-faire personal policy of trying to be what he called in an interview in 1969 "a good Jew."

He became increasingly outraged that certain New York Clubs, such as the Algonquin Club, prohibited Jews from becoming members.

"I just accepted the fact that I wouldn't join certain clubs, that if I was invited to a restricted club it was because my host thought enough of me despite being a Jew," he told one reporter at the time. But as he became more successful he actually began a letter writing campaign to organizations meeting at The Algonquin Club and other "restricted" clubs urging them to boycott these clubs because they excluded Jews. To be sure, Sonnabend ruffled a number of racist feathers but as a result of the new proactive stance he was able to lure a number of galas to The Plaza and away from the restrictive clubs at a time when the hotel urgently needed the additional income for needed repairs and renovations.

The Plaza, despite its New York "400" patrician beginnings, has almost from the start been considerate of all cultures. Perhaps this is a natural result of playing host to all those foreign dignataries. For just one example, The Plaza — long before airlines provided Kosher meals routinely — prided itself on catering to guests' special food preparation needs and desires. But it went beyond its usual attentiveness in 1966 when then Israeli President Shneour Zalman Shazar requested never-before-used silverware be sent to his suite in addition to the hotel having the caterer hire a Mashgiach to oversee Kosher meals.

The Plaza is where many East Coast establishment politicians got their first glimpse of the Ronald Reagan charisma and ideological political machine up close. In a speech in the Grand Ballroom of The Plaza in June 1969, then California Governor Reagan called "economic progress" his top priority and vowed to keep fighting campus violence with force. "In California, we found that it was necessary to bring whatever force is required to restore law and order," he told guests.

Of course, things had gotten a little quieter at Columbia and New York college campuses in the year preceding Reagan's visit. In January 1968, thirty-three protesters outside The Plaza were arrested as they tried to stop a speech of then U.S. Vice President Hubert Humphrey at a gala to benefit the International Institute of Education. Two of the most prominent people who attended Humphrey's speech were Paul Newman and Joanne Woodward. Newman went on to become one of President Nixon's most outspoken critics and very proud of being high up on the infamous "enemies list."

※

Phil Hughes, who became manager of The Plaza in 1976 after Westin Hotels bought it in 1974, replaced Joe Mogush, who was a vice-president of Westin, and Hughes stayed in the job until 1984. Hughes eventually fell in love with Regina Henry, who was public relations director of the hotel during his tenure and they live together in New York today. One of the most eventful things that happened at The Plaza two years after he took over was the FBI ABSCAM sting operation, which took place in one of the suites. U.S. Senator Harrison Williams and others were caught on tape peddling influence.

"An agent from the FBI called me — he had worked for Westin Hotels — and wanted a suite," Hughes told me. "They dressed up as Arab bigwigs and snared a couple of the politicians. We put them up in a suite and they took the connecting door off and made it into a see-through door. But when they called me on it they didn't tell me what it was for. They just said they needed to rent a suite and rent it every weekend. I said it would be difficult to get a guest out who wanted to stay on the weekend and they said, 'We'll just go ahead and pay for every weekend in advance and put it in our name.' So I set it up for that suite to be rented every weekend and they prepaid it all. And then after about four months, my friend in the FBI calls me and says, 'Thank you very much. We've done our business.' And I said, 'I hope we don't get a lot of publicity on this.' And the next day there were the headlines about The Plaza being where the ABSCAM sting operation took place!"

By early 1982, seven members of Congress had been convicted for taking bribes in the FBI's ABSCAM probe in which FBI agents posed as representatives of rich Arabs and offered brides to officials as a hidden camera at The Plaza looked on.

One Congressman even stuffed wads of cash into his pockets. U.S. Senator Williams of New Jersey was also convicted of bribery and sentenced to three years in prison all the while vigorously maintaining his innocence. "I will always steadfastly believe and maintain that I never used my office corruptly," he told a Senate Ethics Committee. "I never sought or received personal gain and never intended to do anything illegal." However, Williams was charged with trying to get a loan from the bogus Arab reps for a mining company in which he had a financial interest.

Grasping at straws in his defense, Williams also said that FBI agents had tried to intoxicate him so that he "would act as they wanted when in front of a hidden camera" at The Plaza.

But Senator Williams was not the only high-ranking member of Congress to play hanky panky at The Plaza, and far from the most famous.

Judith Exner, a beautiful Los Angeles woman who also had a passionate affair with organized crime chieftain, Sam Giancana, met then U.S. Senator John F. Kennedy in Las Vegas in February 1960 when she was dining with Frank Sinatra at the Sands Hotel. According to her autobiography *Judith Exner: My Story*, Kennedy later called her to make a lunch date and they talked frequently on the phone during the time he was campaigning for the Democratic Party nomination for President. But she says in the book that it wasn't until the eve of the New Hampshire primary that they first made love and it was in room 1671 of The Plaza.

She describes herself as suddenly resisting his advances. "All of a sudden . . . I just didn't want what was happening to happen"; and she quotes Kennedy as replying, "Don't misunderstand this. I don't mean to be impatient. I know it probably looks that way, but I have been anticipating this moment for a long time. This has been the longest month . . . I have so looked forward to being close to you, to making love to you and then just lie in bed and talk the way two people can talk after making love."

She continues, without going into graphic detail, that they made love and Kennedy left her room later that night. "What a delight it was to be awakened by a bellman with a dozen roses. The card said, 'Thinking of you — J.' And then to hear that he had won in New Hampshire made it complete."

She said she continued to see Kennedy sporadically after he was elected President at the White House and they were again alone together at The Plaza — this time, she wrote, in suite 1529-31 in the summer of 1961.

"Even Jack was impressed with the size of the suite," she writes in her book. "'I could hide in it for a week. I must say this is an improvement on the first night I was here [at The Plaza.] There's room to breathe.' He toured the whole place, inspected the kitchen, bounced on the bed, stretched out on the living room sofa and nibbled on the hors d'oeuves. . . . We kidded and kissed and as we grew more passionate love took its natural course — at the right moment we just naturally flowed into the bedroom."

James W. Hilty's book *Robert Kennedy* talks about JFK's two-year affair with Judith Campbell Exner without mentioning The Plaza. According to Hilty's book, Campbell claimed she carried messages between Kennedy and Mafia chieftain Sam Giancana, with whom she was also having an affair, concerning buying votes in the important West Virginia Democratic primary election in that state. JFK's affair with Exner apparently abruptly ended, Hilty says, when J. Edgar Hoover, who also loved to stay at The Plaza when he was in New York, was investigating organized crime and threatened to leak news of JFK's relationship with Exner, and the Giancana connection. Their affair is referred to by other biographers as well.

Jackie O. put in her appearances at the hotel, too. Most unusual of all perhaps was during the big blackout of November 9, 1965, that caused almost everything else in the city to come to a standstill, including New York Harbor and subway trains caught in tunnels below ground. *The New York Times* came out the following day but it was an abbreviated edition. A raft of important business conferences were canceled. But Fairfax Cone, executive co-chairman of the advertising firm of Foote, Cone & Belding gave a keynote speech to the Magazine Promotion Group at The Plaza and Jackie Kennedy was escorted by Franklin D. Roosevelt, Jr. to the world premier of *The Eleanor Roosevelt Story* and the Cinema Rendezvous on 57th Street followed by an after-theater supper in The Plaza's Persian Room.

The Plaza handled the blackout with a sense of style and elegence befitting the world's ultimate hotel. The Oak Room served roast beef sandwiches by candlelight and people in the hotel without rooms were permitted to spend the night in the lobby and staircases. The gas-fired stoves in The Plaza kitchen were able to produce light meals including rare roast beef for some Plaza patrons who were roughing it in the candlelit Edwardian Room. Upstairs in the Grand Ballroom a fashion show was in progress and, without missing a beat, a gorgeous model came down the runway just after the spotlights went out illuminated by a single candle she was cradling in her hands.

The Plaza-Kennedy association has one more sensational chapter. In his book *Greek Fire: The Story of Maria Callas and Aristotle Onassis*, former *New York Times* investigative reporter Nicholas Gage says that within weeks of his marriage to Jackie Kennedy on October 20, 1968, Onassis was seeing his old paramour Maria Callas. And, in fact, Onassis, who tried to keep courtship of Jackie secret, took elaborate measures to continue to see Callas during the courtship, and after he married Jackie, at the time Callas was living in a large suite at The Plaza, (rent free) and around the time teaching her "Master Class" on opera at the Julliard School for Music at Lincoln Center.

Geraldine Sheppard, who did public relations for The Plaza in the late 1960s, told me, "Onassis was there at The Plaza and calling her all the time because his calls came through me. He was there. He would come up to her suite all the time."

About Callas herself, Sheppard, now in real estate, said: "She was fabulous. She was absolutely fabulous . . . And Onassis never got over her.

"Her suite was given to her," Sheppard elaborates. "A lot of celebrities were given rooms in those days. But she hated the first suite we had given her and I was taking drawers of her clothes out of one suite and taking them to the other suite which was on Central Park. It was really a crummy, run-down suite she was first put in. And she had to have her special pillows and her maid and she lived there for quite a while when she taught at Julliard."

Callas taught a total of twenty-six master classes at the Julliard School of Music from October 11, 1971 to March 16, 1972. By the way, Geraldine Sheppard is also the sister of prominent New York socialite Patricia Patterson, who was married to industrialist Bruce Norris, who once had a financial interest in The Plaza before Westin took it over in the mid-1970s.

In his book on Callas and Onassis, Nicholas Gage states that Callas was so upset with Onassis after he married Jackie Kennedy that Callas vowed she'd never sleep with him again. Gage quotes a friend of the diva's as saying Callas told her she would "Never!" sleep with him as long as they were married. But hotel sources believe — but of course can't prove — that Onassis's visits to Callas' suite were not merely platonic, her protestations aside. Onassis's plans to divorce Jackie, who shunned his cronies and surpassed even his gargantuan spending habits, were abruptly set aside when his son Alexander was killed the following year piloting his private plane on takeoff from Athens Airport in January 1973.

Long before he met Jackie Kennedy, Aristotle Onassis met his first wife, Tina, at a diner party at The Plaza on April 17, 1943. He would later inscribe a bracelet of Alexander the Great coins with the date. After divorcing Tina and marrying Jackie Kennedy, Onassis liked nothing more than a casual dinner at Trader Vic's and in February, 1969, photographers snapped the couple while Jackie sipped a Tahitian coffee and John F. Kennedy Jr. scooped up a handful of fortune cookies. Jackie and her late husband, then U.S. Senator John F. Kennedy, came to The Plaza the year before he became President when on December 8, 1959 they attended a benefit for the Joseph P. Kennedy Jr. Foundation, which provided money for pre-school education.

※

J. Edgar Hoover had, according to one source, his own scandalous behavior at The Plaza. The longtime head Fed may have provoked fear into the hearts of the "Most Wanted" of his day but some of his visits to The Plaza in the late 1950s have overtones of a Charles Busch stage comedy. Susan Rosenstiel, who was once married to Schenley liquor baron Lewis Solon Rosenstiel, told Hoover biographer Anthony Summers, in his *Official and Confidential: The Secret Life of J. Edgar Hoover*, that on one occasion she visited the heavyset Hoover in his Plaza suite to find he "was wearing a fluffy black dress, very fluffy, with flounces, and lace stockings and high heels. He had makeup on and false eyelashes. It was a very short skirt, and he was sitting there in the living room of the suite with his legs crossed. Roy [Roy Cohn, the lawyer and a Lewis Rosenstiel associate] introduced him to me as 'Mary' and he replied, 'Good evening,' brusque like the first time I met him. It was obvious he wasn't a woman, you could see where he shaved. It was Hoover. You've never seen anything like it. I couldn't believe it, that I should see the head of the FBI dressed as a woman."

Rosenstiel also told Summers that the following year she again was invited by her husband, an old friend of Hoover's, to go to Hoover's Plaza suite and the FBI director was even more flamboyantly dressed.

"He had a red dress on and a black feather boa around his neck," Summers quotes Rosenstiel. Summers also says Rosenstiel signed a sworn affidavit that there was no mistaking that Hoover was the fellow in the fluffy back dress and the red one with the boa.

Behind the Front Desk — Getting Personal With the Personnel

elieve it or not, there are people who know, and love, The Plaza Hotel far better than me. The everyday people who work there.

Perhaps the most important statement from any Plaza manager was by Alfonse Salomone (yes, that same man who thought Eloise was a nuisance), who died at the age of 73 in 1993. Salomone, who had started his career as a desk clerk in a hotel in Knoxville, Tennessee, said: "People have, when they leave a hotel, a receipted bill and a memory." It was the memory part, Salomone urged his employees, that really made the difference.

It was also Salomone who was very candid about the hotel almost not making it to the end of the 20th Century. "This old girl was on the verge of being torn down," he admonished in a 1960 interview, when he helped rescue The Plaza from dwindling occupancy and revenue. As the hotel's acting managing director and the Vice President of its parent company, The Hotel Corporation of America, it was Salomone who directed its restoration.

But something of this kind happened time and time again with the hotel. In fact, it was on the verge of almost being torn down several times. Some of this speculation was undoubtedly hyperbole; but another part was undeniable fact.

To hear it from Philip Hughes, some years after Salomone left the hotel (during the years when Westin owned The Plaza in the 1970's and early 1980's) "the great gray lady" was "on borrowed time."

Of course, many things helped save The Plaza, from a Saudi Arabian Prince to an upsurge in the economy. But at least on a subconscious level The Plaza has had one thing going for it since the beginning: Central Park. Few people ever imagine Central Park without its glorious Plaza backdrop, that whitebrick castle-like structure with the green mansard roof. But just as important are the hotel's employees who often have treated The Plaza as their very own.

"Everyone who passes through here and has the privilege of working here certainly has to be humbled by the 94-year history," says Gary Schweikert. "You feel like you're a small piece of a much bigger, greater thing. And that gives people a sense of belonging."

Highly respected New York City public relations woman Regina Henry, who spent five years as head of public relations for The Plaza, says the elegant circle of hotels in the blocks around The Plaza are unique in American cities and breed a special loyalty among their workers. "Hotels have always been like the center of activity in their respective cities or town," says Henry. "It just so happens that these hotels are in the greatest city in the world and 'midtown' in the greatest city in the world. So that lends an aura of romance and a specialness, a uniqueness and the people who are attracted to work there are aware of that. That these are special buildings in a special place; you do get caught up in that atmosphere.

"And there are people in the community, within five or ten blocks from the hotel who think of The Plaza or other hotels in midtown as 'their' hotel. They go for tea in the afternoon or for lunch or Mother's Day brunch. So there's a local community as well as a global community that feels very proprietary." To

Henry, there's as much "romance" involved with the employees serving the guests in various capacities as guests have celebrating anniversaries, concluding major business deals and spending their honeymoon at the grand hotel.

Henry thinks of The Plaza "being like a small town because it's so self-contained. Maybe it's not quite the butcher, the baker and the candlestick maker but it is a full pastry department, a kitchen, a laundry; they run all their own services. You get to know all the people who combine to make this a positive experience for a guest. In that respect there really is a great sense of romance, not only for the guests who you hope are there enjoying the total 'guest' experience but for the people working there, too. What satisfaction to be a part of a team which delivers a whole product to a guest."

"For me," says Plaza General Manager Gary Schweikert, "it's hard even to imagine what could be better than this. It's really hard. Our business, really, is the next best thing to being in the theater. We're setting the stage for people, for real people. When they come here, they're the actors on the stage, and the stage is this grand old hotel."

Jeffrey Jacobs is The Plaza director of food and beverage, in charge of some 500 employees, including chefs, banquet managers, restaurant managers, waiters and the like. He has his own tales of Plaza magic: "The Palm Court opened originally as a tea room, and our tea is very famous. People from all over the world come to have tea at The Plaza Hotel. Celebrities as well as tourists. And their expectation of it is not about tea, not about the room; it's about the experience. The Plaza experience is kind of like that movie *The Way We Were* with Robert Redford and Barbra Streisand where they are discovering what is great in life, that the elegance and style of a bygone era is something they have to experience. The Challenge that those of us who work here have is — we don't want to do it only on special occasions. We want to do it all the time. . . . We want to meet customers' expectations by having great food, a great experience, in an ambiance that is suspended in time, like The Ritz and The Savoy in London or The Crillion in Paris. Places that you wouldn't think of as changing, that you would never want to change. So when a customer comes in here or a celebrity comes in here they know exactly what they want; they're coming in here and they're saying, 'Wow! This is The Plaza Hotel.'

"This room [The Palm Court], for instance. My daughters have a word for it. They say it's a 'magical' room. It's a restaurant but it's a magical room. It's almost like being lost in time, but top of the line. The best. My children say, 'Royalty used to go there. Why can't I experience what royalty used to experience?'"

***

Every once in a while the New York City tabloid newspapers print a "good news" story about an honest taxi driver or messenger who finds a wallet stuffed with cash and returns it to its rightful owner without thought of reward. The Plaza is no stranger to this type of story. Such as the time one of their chambermaids, who had herself once lost a passport, her only identification, literally didn't think twice about all the cash she found in a billfold one day.

Her name is Nora Sullivan and in 1963 she found a wallet in a top drawer with a lot of money and two passports. Taking them immediately to her boss, head housekeeper Kay Arendt, she exclaimed that the man with the missing wallet will be in "the devils own mess without these passports."

"But did you see all this money?" Arendt asked.

"Yes, yes, but it's the passports that's important," Sullivan went on.

The owner was eventually found back home in Texas and he generously gave Sullivan the cash contents of the wallet of over $500. Subsequently interviewed by a local reporter and asked if she was ever tempted to take the money, Sullivan said "Oh, no, no. It's part of our religion to be honest."

***

Paul Nicaj, former Executive Director of Banquets, has seen and heard it all. He has been, as has been discussed, with the King of Morocco as well as with people who have come to their functions in blue jeans and uncombed hair. "The one with blue jeans turned out to be one of the most expensive parties." He's had people in their twenties and people in their eighties: "I had a wedding where the grandmother died in the middle of the dance floor, dancing, at the age of 82. Nice death, nice way to go. And you sort of got to hide that. And I told the people, we put her aside, and I said she's resting in the rooms, she's fine, just tired, That's what I told the father of the bride because it was on the groom's side.

"If you want perfection and satisfaction, you should be there four hours before the function, and most functions last eight hours, and then you should always be there to thank them and say goodnight to them. They remember if you do."

Besides the Grand Ballroom, the heart and soul of The Plaza's function rooms, which comprised Nicaj's world, are on the second floor, beginning with the series of long rectangular suites facing Central Park called Versailles A & B facing Fifth Avenue and walking clockwise around the hotel. La Suite Fragonard, a much smaller suite, is at the corner of Fifth Avenue and 58th Street. Along 58th Street, going from East to West, there's L'Hermitage A & B, La Suite Louis XV A & B, followed by the Grand Ballroom foyer and the Grand Ballroom on the west side of the hotel. It is followed by the almost equally mammoth Baroque Room, and then along Central Park South the White and Gold Rooms, A, B, & C. Lastly, at the Central Park South and Fifth Avenue corner the State Suite and next to it, just before the Versailles Suite, the tiny Blue Room.

The State Suite like many of the other large, grandiose suites on the hotel's second floor started out life not as a function room but as a "regular" guest room, rented out like any other. One early occupant of the State Suite (it is believed) was the wealthy young Duke Franz Joseph of Bavaria (Franz Joseph Michael Karl Maria Evarist Quirinus Ottokar to be exact), the brother of Queen Elisabeth of Belguim. For a young European nobleman, Franz expressed much enthusiasm for American capitalism and oddly, for his station and times, the good old American work ethic.

"After I complete my present term of service I shall visit America again. I think it is much better for one to have work he is interested in. I love work; I could never be idle. I think when you are engaged in some sort of work that life is much more satisfactory," the Duke told one interviewer in August 1910 in his sumptuous Plaza suite. "I should like very much, I think, to return here when I complete my army service and enter the banking business."

The Duke went on to say that, while he'd brought his guns along to "do some shooting in the West," he wasn't also hunting for a bride. "I do not know that I shall meet many ladies here," he offered, adding that he'd, "go to Newport for a short visit, and meet Mrs. Robert Goelet and a few others."

The Duke's plans to become a banker were, alas, cut short when he died two years later on September 23, 1912.

"When I come in, in the morning," Nicaj resumes, "I go behind the scenes, looking at the people as they start; from potato peeler to the porter to the dishwasher, people who have to make the room beautiful. I know very well that it happens from those people. Unfortunately, it's very rarely recognized. I always try to recognize it. When I get thanked for weddings, those people don't hear it, but I always make sure they do. In essence, one has an obligation as a boss to treat your staff fairly and as if they are important. Not only will you make friends that way, but also you will get better work from your workers."

At one particular moment in the interview, we were discussing what it meant to be a king or a princess or prince. Nicaj said, "I respect titles and I respect customs because if it means something to them, why should I knock it? As long as it doesn't hurt the society, it doesn't bother me. But, when a few titles bring a function, it's fine." He laughs. "They want to honor someone who is a king, it's fine, as long as they do it in the Ballroom with four hundred people; even better!"

Nicaj has had his share of kings too. There was one time when he had to meet with the King and Queen of Sweden.

"I tell you a funny story I never told anybody ever about. I, and this director of marketing, had to wait for them (the King and Queen) on Fifth Avenue. I was more tense and younger and nervous, and I had to greet them as they came into the hotel. They wanted somebody in a tuxedo and young, and so they put somebody — in the middle of the day — in a tuxe-do . . . they got me.

"And, the director of marketing at the time was from Denmark, a guy by the name of Hans Brasse. They were preparing me and teaching me how to be a waiter, and to say, 'Your Royal Highness, welcome to the hotel; Your Majesty, wel-come to the hotel.' And I practiced and practiced . . . how con-fused I got! When the King and Queen arrived, I said, 'Your Highness, and then I called her the Majesty, and then I caught myself. The king actually made a joke; he was a nice man — he says, 'It's all confusing.'" Nicaj laughs again. "They didn't tell me who was going to walk in first!"

Nicaj told another funny story concerning a function he supervised: "We lost a salad for four hundred people, in one of the elevators. The kitchen area is so big and the cook had just started two days before that, and they told him to send the salad to the Ballroom. He had forgotten which elevator, we have so many that go to different areas, and by the time the speeches have to be done and by the time the salad would be found; forget it! It's like every business, things happen. We found the salad when the dessert was served — just too late."

※

George Lang, culinary genius and owner of New York's Café Des Artists, was a "saucier" at The Plaza long before he became an executive in the banquet department of The Waldorf-Astoria.

Born in Hungary, Lang had two passions as a boy: food and

the violin. He came to New York to become a music professional. His heart was in food. "I decided to give up the violin as
a profession," he told me in his office, which looks like a
branch of the public library, on Manhattan's West 67th Street,
"and to slowly and completely get into the hospitality industry.
I went down to the state employment agency and then to about
a hundred employment agencies located on two floors near the
state agency — and within two hours, you could be rejected by
every one of them! It would reduce almost anyone, regardless
of their security or size or ego, to a non-person. Finally, at one
place, a nice gentleman talked to me. He was the first humane
person, instead of someone barking at me, saying 'Show me
your credentials!' which I didn't have."

That "humane person" sent him to a restaurant on West
57th Street. But Lang had to leave this kitchen assignment
hastily when the chef one day came running after him with a
carving knife. Lang, who couldn't speak much English then,
misunderstood the chef who handed him a plateful of delicious
seafood. He raced downstairs to the basement and devoured it
in two minutes flat. A friend flew down the stairs yelling the
chef was "looking for you. He wants to kill you." The seafood
was for Claudette Colbert.

Years later, Lang was running the Four Seasons restaurant
when Colbert came for dinner. He presented her with a reprise
of that long-forgotten platter of seafood and told her why.

In his wonderful memoir, *Nobody Knows The Truffles I've Seen*,
Lang writes his "excitement was hard to contain" when he first
started working in the kitchen of The Plaza in 1953.

"Working in such a super-organized kitchen as The Plaza's,
where each department was an autonomous entity, yet inde-
pendent with the others, I learned how to create systems that
became a basic tool in my profession later as a consultant," he
writes. "To learn as much as possible, I worked for (or at least
watched) some of the fine craftsmen at The Plaza's kitchens,
such as Aldo Fattori, the chef garde-manager of an especially
gifted brigade, and I would stay many hours after my shift was

over, furiously taking notes.

"Top professionals in many disciplines like to dazzle each other with pointless technical tricks. I learned, for instance, how to make a *pomme en cage*, an imprisoned potato ball within a potato cube carved out of a single potato. After I perfected this arcane skill, I used to frighten young apprentices by telling them they must make a couple of dozen to be fried for a party of ten within thirty minutes.

"Those were the days when superannuated dowagers lived in plush suites at The Plaza and would give recipes to the room-service manager, who in turn passed them on to the chef, and we had to prepare these dishes to be served in their parlors. I had to cook, for instance, a breast of baby chicken, cut into precisely half-inch cubes, in a light cream sauce and put into a specially baked, hollowed-out, large-sized brioche — exactly at 6:00 P.M., to be served to one old lady by selected room service waiters at 6:15 several times a week."

❋

During one previous foray into The Plaza's subbasement I ran across Vito Belfuri. Now retired, he was the hotel's head carpenter as well as a sort of walking "back-of-the-house" archive. Vito had been with the hotel for more than 30 years and saw many people, managers included, come and go.

Interviewing Vito in his shop in the subbasement was like being back at woodworking class in high school. All round him in meticulously neat piles were different lengths of wood. And when something was out of place, when a chair needed repairing or a doorknob replaced, Vito was the first one people called.

As gifted and respectful of The Plaza as its managers have been over the years they wouldn't have much success without the accouterments of the hotel itself, which may have been remodeled and reconfigured but never lost their essential character. Largely thanks to the efforts of craftsmen like Vito.

"Like the State Suite on the Central Park and Fifth Avenue Corner of The Plaza," Vito offers in example, "which was designed in the style of Louis the XIV."

King Louis should have been so lucky as to have Vito and his tools around.

⌗

Philip Hughes, Plaza General Manager from 1976 to 1984, inaugurated the ad campaign "Nothing unimportant happens at The Plaza." This, of course, has many meanings to many people. It can range from the biggest debutante ball to an important state department dinner to, simply, tourists gawking at the crystal chandeliers and marble hallways.

Before Trump brought in Barry Cregan, few Plaza managers were as "hands on" with celebrity guests as Richard Wilhelm, as ruggedly good-looking as some of his celebrity guests. Wilhelm had been a top executive at The Waldorf-Astoria before moving to The Plaza when Donald Trump bought the hotel in 1988. Wilhelm took a lot of pride in personally serving some of his better known guests, escorting them to their suites and recalling their preferences for food and drink.

"Joel Silver, the producer of the Bruce Willis [action] films and others, has stayed with us for several weeks at a time and we know his requirements," Wilhelm recalled over a lunch in The Peninsula Hotel. "He's extremely nice. David Goldberg, the producer of the TV series *Brooklyn Bridge* among others, has stayed with us. He enjoyed it. He told a lot of other people in L.A. about us. So one day we had the pastry chef make up a spun sugar and chocolate Brooklyn Bridge. And when he and his wife arrived we brought it up to his suite and they really enjoyed it. I remember once we had a birthday cake for Joel Silver and we had some of the chefs go up to his suite and sing happy birthday to him.

"Madonna was a frequent visitor when Warren Beatty stayed with us," Wilhelm continued. "Beatty stayed with us for a whole week when he was doing the opening of *Dick Tracy* and had to go to several premieres in Boston and Orlando and so forth. He stayed with us and just jetted in and out of New York."

⊠

Over the years, the kind of food The Plaza has served has changed dramatically as people have become more health and weight conscious. But the responsibilities of the hotel's executive chef, who's in charge of a small army of more than a hundred chefs and cooks, has remained virtually the same.

Daily, thousands of meals come out of The Plaza's kitchen that takes up most of the basement and some of the space on the first and the second floor, which is also the banquet floor. There's the Oak Room, One C.P.S. (formerly The Edwardian Room) overlooking Central Park, the Oyster Bar, and of course, the Palm Court, which serves more formal teas than any other restaurant in New York and at holiday times has a line of people waiting to get in literally a block long. Then there are all the weddings and banquets and smaller functions and a room service production line that makes a Busby Berkeley musical seem like a high school pageant in comparison.

And it takes a lot more than knowledge of food and a track record as a chef to be in charge of such operations. It takes a military-like discipline with the drive of a Broadway director and the figurative balance, under extremes, of a ballet dancer. In football terms, the executive chef has to be coach, quarterback and be part of the cheering section all rolled into one.

It was a beautiful late spring day when I drove up New York State's Taconic Parkway to visit Joseph Trombetti, who more than any other chef, had been associated with The Plaza Hotel and had held the job of executive chef longer than anyone else.

In a rustic house that was as much unlike the elegant exterior or public space interiors of the hotel as The Plaza kitchens where he worked so many years, I found Trombetti and his wife of 43 years.

The Trombettis retired to a home near Route 9 in a house not far from the picturesque Hudson River and Rhinebeck,

New York. The only connection the simple wood-frame house had with The Plaza was the numerous awards that adorned its walls.

Before us on the dinner table was a delicious fish and lobster stew, the likes of which I never had tasted before or since. To say it was rich is to say Donald Trump has a few bucks tucked away. It seemed to me, especially after nearly a three-hour drive, to be like eating melted lobster and scallops mixed together.

Somewhat less appetizing, there were also mounted trophies of animals from squirrels to woodchucks on the walls. Trombetti loves to hunt when he isn't cooking — although, mercifully, he doesn't always cook what he hunts.

The executive chef had retired several years earlier because, frankly, he'd had it. His job was like waging a battle every day, he told me.

Born in Parma in Northern Italy, young Trombetti learned his basic culinary skills from his uncle who was also an executive chef. He went on to know much about Northern Italian cooking but very little about that of Southern Italy. It wouldn't be until after he came to America at the age of 19 that he would add Southern Italian cooking to his growing repertoire.

At age 26, he came to The Plaza as a roast cook. The year was 1957. After being promoted to Chef Saucier two years later he continued to get promotions in The Plaza kitchen and was named executive chef in 1971. While he said he learned much from visiting restaurants both in Europe and in New York, The Plaza's menu didn't change dramatically from year to year the way some menus did.

"The Plaza became unique because its cuisine remained traditional," he said. "I liked to add some nouvelle cuisine to the menu, for variety's sake, but The Plaza's cooking was mostly classical and that is getting rare. Suddenly a new style came in and all the restaurants in New York converted. The distinction is one of the reasons The Plaza's restaurants continued to be so popular.

"I get ideas when I'm in Europe. and I make it a point to visit restaurants here in town once in a while, particularly when a new one is making a splash."

About four times a year, Chef Trombetti would sit down and decide what changes to make to The Plaza's menus. Summer cooking, he says, is a challenge. Fruits and vegetables must be carefully chosen — ripe enough, but not overripe, unbruised from shipping; recently picked; and prepared and served while still fresh.

"Cold soups and cold salads are more difficult to prepare than hot dishes," Trombetti explains. "They depend on the absolute freshness and the quality of each ingredient for their flavor, often without the art of releasing or blending their flavors through various kinds of cooking. Also, there has to be a wide variety of choices, because salads can be boring after awhile."

One morning, in a carefree mood, Chef Trombetti decided to slip Rosselnik (cold cucumber) soup on the menu along with a seafood salad, two long-popular summer favorites at The Plaza. "Its decor, as you know, is warm and clubby, with dark wood paneling and heavy furnishings," he said. "You have to take that into consideration when choosing the menu. Too much heavy food can be overwhelming. You enjoy both the decor and the meal more when they complement each other."

His experiment, not surprisingly, was a big hit.

※

Executive chef Bruno Rene Tison, who we have already made the acquaintance of during our virtual tour, was classically trained in France and incorporates his style with American cuisine. Chef Tison trained with several of France's master chefs, including Bernard Waterlot, Roger Verge, Michael Guerard, and Main Chapel.

Before becoming Executive Chef at The Plaza Hotel, he was Executive Chef at the Beau Geste, New York, where one critic said, "Chef Tison has a firm grasp of color, taste, and texture that produces a wide range of interestingly flavorful tastes." He was also Executive Chef of the five-star Ernie's Restaurant, San Francisco, and Chef de Cuisine at Pierre Meridian, San Francisco, where he oversaw all facets of Main Chapel's first American restaurant.

"Even when I'm taking a training course I'm still representing The Plaza," Tison told me several years ago over lunch in the Edwardian Room, (now One C.P.S.) "I took one such course at The Crillion in Paris and to me The Ritz in Paris and The Crillion are the finest hotels in the world. The food at The Crillion is so magnificent. The service is just unbelievable. Not only in the restaurants, but all around the hotel. In the dining room of The Crillion alone you have from twenty-five to forty service people at any one time. We can't compete in America. The price of a dinner in 1990 at the Crillion was $300 per person. The cheapest bottle of wine was $100. I was there for the experience and the research. But I had to be careful. Because it's difficult to compare the two properties, The Crillion and The Plaza.

"At The Plaza we service from between 2000 and 6000 people a day, including banquets. When I eat in a restaurant in The Plaza I give my comments the next day, such as "It was not what we discussed," or some such. And the next day I'm in the restaurant again and order the same thing again. Individual chefs know that I'm responsible for a certain standard and style.

"I personally oversee the entire culinary department of The Plaza Hotel restaurants. I've selected a chef and a sous chef who will give exactly what we want in each restaurant, I really give a lot of freedom to each chef. My role as executive chef is to make sure my people provide the best food available. My background had never been a hotel background. For over twelve years in France I worked with three-star chefs. This is the kind of background I have. And I know exactly what a signature chef wants to do; it would be very, very embarrassing if I would write a menu and just hand it to each chef. So what basically we do is I usually get with my supervisors, the general manager, the food and beverage director and we decide which direction we want to take each restaurant.

"The chef of the Edwardian Room knows I am responsible for a certain structure and certain guidelines and he really helps me with that and I really help him in giving him the maximum of freedom in his cuisine. Now we have to work together. We have to put together a menu that's functional for the Edwardian Room and also for The Plaza Hotel. In the Edwardian Room we have to be extremely careful in what we're doing. We have to be a signature restaurant but we also have to take care of our clientele, which is a worldwide, traveled clientele. Thirty-five to 40 percent is from mid-America and we have to take care of these people. We have to accommodate them. Of course, we have three more restaurants. We have the Palm Court, we have the Oyster Bar and we have the Oak Room.

"Imagine someone coming from the Middle East and they are staying at The Plaza and want to eat at the signature restaurant. And they are sitting beside someone who has not been exposed to nouvelle cuisine or very international cuisine, and wants to enjoy the service and dining experience of the Oak Room and still order chicken potpie. So we have to be very careful we accommodate both kinds of clientele.

"We want the Oak Room to have the comfort, luxury and service of the finest restaurant in the city and yet if a guest wants to eat a hamburger we will provide it even if it's not on our menu. It's a service-oriented profession.

"We are a hotel and being a hotel we have to please the guest while he or she is staying at The Plaza. From the minute the guest walks in we have to make sure he's very well taken care of. It's much, much more difficult to be the chef of a hotel or chef of a restaurant in a hotel in New York City than a chef in a restaurant. They don't have to deal with unions and the regulations we have to deal with."

For my lunch with Tison in the Edwardian I ordered the lobster ravioli as an appetizer and the "exotic lamb" as a main course. To my great relief, Chef Tison applauded: "A good choice. A very good choice."

※

Shrimp, not tea sandwiches, were the order of the day at Trader Vic's, which has long since set sail from The Plaza's basement, but is hardly forgotten. It was in its own way, and time, as unique a Plaza feature as the Persian Room.

The restaurant had been at the Savoy Plaza across the street for years, and opened at The Plaza in April, 1965. In a sneak peek, gossip columnist Suzy Knickerbocher (Aileen Mehle) said, "When Trader Vic's moves from the Savoy Hilton (which Hilton had renamed it when the chain bought the Savoy Plaza) they will use a 54-foot outrigger canoe for decor. It's the same one Marion Brando necked in with native girls while filming *Mutiny on the Bounty*." As it had at the Savoy Plaza, the new Trader Vic's at The Plaza quickly became a hangout for celebrities. Anthony Quinn and gossip columnist Cindy Adams and her husband comedian Joey Adams often ate there together Sunday nights. Vice President and then President Richard M. Nixon loved to go there.

The brains behind Trader Vic's was Victor Bergeron, who began with one restaurant called Hinky Dinks in Oakland, California, where he personally was the chef. Trader Vic's was immensely successful because Victor personally demanded that the best fish, shrimp, beef and vegetables were used. And he was able to ride the crest of Americans' growing love affair with Polynesian and Chinese food and provide them with an Americanized version of it in exotic Polynesian settings.

I got to know him in the early 1980's when I interviewed him for The *Christian Science Monitor* after having dinner with him at Trader Vic's in The Plaza. I wove into the story that he had a wooden leg and over the years had helped many veterans who had lost legs in combat — something he really never talked about. He later told me he appreciated how I took him seriously as a restaurateur and entrepreneur and not just a "character" who had struck it rich reinventing Polynesian food for the American palate.

He also gave me his card with a note scribbled on it which he said would entitle me and any number of guests I chose to bring with me to dinner at any Trader Vic's in the country. When I presented it to the somewhat confused manager of the Trader Vic's in Dallas he said, "Oh, the boss has been giving out cards again!"

※

Tall, lean, and with an unflappable disposition and graciousness which is honed on the diet of planning marriage receptions, major anniversaries and other major parties, Lawrence Harvey, the Executive Director of Catering at The Plaza, looks like he might as well be at home on the Broadway stage. And, in fact, his "stage" is his comfortable photograph-lined office on the terrace level and 58th Street side of the grand hotel. He's got the impishness and suaveness of a Tony Randall but none of the barbed cynicism. Harvey's is a "what-can-I-do-and-it-can-never-be-too-much-to-serve-you" kind of attitude.

One of the things Harvey seemed to be fond of saying is, "this is my life," as he points to the front portion of his Rolodex files which contained just a few of his many contacts with the rich and famous (and, the rich who want to be famous). This coming from a man who looks as if he just walked out of a Noël Coward play — impeccably relaxed amid the swirling chaos of this or that social whirl. Lawrence Harvey is a breath of fresh Mediterranean air in an exclusive world, which is all in a tizzy with trials and tribulations of a father trying to get their daughter or son married off.

Harvey's style is really what makes The Plaza the elegant place it is. Basically, his distinct style is to be extremely honest and truthful — no matter how much money someone has to spend or how low they are on the social ladder.

It was mid-morning, two days before "the wedding." Lawrence Harvey, The Plaza's director of catering, was remarkably relaxed. He certainly had reason to be relaxed; in the top world of catering in which he is preeminent, there is reason why. He is the best. He had learned his craft well and, five years before, had been wooed away from his lucrative and secure position as the director of catering of The Waldorf-Astoria to join Donald and, then wife, Ivana Trump, in their attempt to revitalize The Plaza.

The Trumps finally got their man, in 1988, when Harvey "moved" over to The Plaza. Westin Hotels had expended an estimated $40 million on the property, but it was not enough to completely restore the hotel.

"The physical condition of some of the guest rooms, public areas and the lobby was very, very bad," Harvey recalls. "The staff also needed a pick-me-up to renew their pride. I think they needed to see the building re-done for their pride to come back. I really give credit to Mr. Trump' stewardship of the hotel for that.

"I think The Plaza exemplifies the style that everyone would like for their wedding. Not everyone can afford to do it in a location such as this, but if they are going any place around the country, this could be the ultimate standard bearer."

Other famous weddings and/or wedding receptions at The Plaza include the Mercedes Kellogg-Sid Bass, and Princess Yasmin Aga Khan. The Robert Goulet-Carol Lawrence wedding and Julie Nixon-David Eisenhower wedding reception.

"Many people who come in don't know what they are doing," Harvey said. "Many people do know a tremendous amount about what they are doing. My job is to decipher which is the case and make them look extremely good. In turn, you develop a client loyalty and they stick with you.

"My motto is you must always be honest. I tell my staff if you don't know something, say you don't know it, but you will find it out. And then, stay with the customer the whole time. One thing I really emphasized with the head waiter staff here — and we went from one to four head waiters — is that when people come into this building, this is their home while they're here. You must do everything as if they were a guest in your home. If you do that, you will have a loyal customer. The next day I call them and write them a hand-written note. Then, I follow with another booking the following year. They sign it, return it, and that's the way you develop that 85 percent client base that comes in year after year."

His advice, after many years in the business, is to never be ashamed of how much you have to spend for a wedding, no matter how little.

"No one should be ashamed of their budget," he states. "But, you should be truthful with it. If money is no object, that is perfectly fine. But, even if it is not an object, we never encourage at this hotel, extravagance beyond belief. Everything should be done with great style and taste. And we always want to know who they are working with. Who the florist is, etc., so we keep everything in style."

What dish stands out to Harvey in The Plaza's weddings?

"Probably rack of lamb. The next most favorite is roast of veal, because that is not as objectionable to most people. If it is, a safe bet is to go back to poultry. Some will go to beef, I really don't have a problem with it, but I think that what you eat in a hotel dining room shouldn't be what you eat every day. It should be special when you come here. I think veal is a very nice choice."

Everyone just calls him Fred. To some, he's Fred of The Plaza, just as there was an "Oscar of the Waldorf." In just over fifty years of serving celebrities, the maitre'd of The Plaza's Oak Room, where he still works one or two days a week, has come a long way since he was earlier known to be like one of the Dead End Kids in the Sidney Kingsley's play of the same name. But, even with his harsh background, Fred was a good boy.

Fred Cristina is and has always been just plain Fred to just about everyone of the customers he has come into contact with. From the India fabric kings to former Broadway actor

Jimmy Cagney, who, of course, became a film star of some note.

In essence, Fred, was like a railroad traffic agent in the old days. His "tower" was a Maitre d's desk and from there he tried to make sure the Cagneys, Grants, Wonders, etc., didn't derail and made it securely into their own particular sidings.

Fred has put on many different masks. Maitre d', waiter, busboy. You name it, Fred has done it. But, what about his family life? Fred, ironically, met his wife at the hotel. She was working for a glove factory for quite some time, but she eventually found it too boring. So she moved over to hats — she became a Plaza hat-check girl, where she found that Fred fit her like a glove as a lifelong mate. The two had one daughter and his wife eventually retired to take care of her while Fred worked two jobs to keep afloat.

"Cagney was a very distinguished looking man; serious man," Fred harks back. We were ensconced, thanks to Fred's connections, in the Cohan Corner of the Oak Room. "When you see the movie *Yankee Doodle Dandy* with Jimmy Cagney, I assume Cagney was that way in his younger years. Because, don't forget, at the time that he was coming here, he went up and then all of a sudden he was coming down. [He would] stand right there, maybe have one or two drinks then take off. Smoke a cigarette. Many an evening he used to hang out with old-time Broadway star William Gaxton and Victor Moore (who at the time was doing *Anything Goes* with Ethel Merman)."

Fred has seen them all. Stevie Wonder, in particular, is his newest favorite.

"Stevie Wonder comes in here all the time. One time, he came in at closing and I opened the room for him. He played a new song he'd written just for us."

Not only has he talked to and seen different celebrities perform for him (others include such greats as Connie Stevens, Al Pacino, Raymond Burr and Orson Welles, who'd just wrapped a little film by the name of *Citizen Kane*), Fred has himself performed in several film productions, including *Regarding Henry* with Harrison Ford, *Arthur*, and with Mia Farrow and Robert Redford in *The Great Gatsby*.

"I was on vacation," said Fred of *Arthur*, "and they called me back to set up the Oak Room because they used to close the Oak Room for a few months, and they said, 'Fred, set up the Oak Room for a movie.' The way you see it in the movie, I set that all up. We did a fantastic job, seven days of a ball. Dudley Moore was great. Liza wasn't here, in this scene. The girl he had with him, the hooker? The pair of pants must have been about this wide — tight pants, you know. It was so funny. I told these people, 'You're going to get an Oscar for this.'"

The following spring, Sir John Gielgud won the Oscar for Supporting Actor as Arthur's cynical, ailing, yet compassionate butler. Fred, of course, had been right.

Fred started off his career at a much humbler station. "I was just a busboy. I was working here in a French restaurant, Gaston's La Bonne Soup on 55th Street. There's one there now, but it's not the one. It was four houses west, a French owner name of Gaston.

"I used to go there and clean the sidewalk, in my father's cook pants. And he had given me an apron. My father was a cook. I cleaned windows. I was the only busboy. And, my father took me to Sixth Avenue and bought me a tuxedo without stripes, because everybody wore tuxedos in the restaurant. I walked out of there one afternoon and said what am I doing? My father wanted me to continue in school. I said I want to go to work. My uncles were waiters, Maitre d's, cooks or chefs."

He was born on 46th Street between 2nd and 3rd Avenues. It was only a few short blocks to The Plaza, but to Fred it seemed like a half a world away.

"What I did was I used to pass The Plaza, so one day I walked into the Fifth Avenue side and into the personnel office and there I met the Maitre d', who in those days was in charge of all the five restaurants, and every restaurant had a head waiter. He was very nice. I'll never forget: he sat at the table, had a waiter cooking his lunch for him. I said 'I'd like an application. I'd like to work at The Plaza, a busboy job.' So, he says, 'Why do you want to work at The Plaza?' 'I want to learn the business, I want to become a waiter.'

"And he looks up at me, I'll never forget, 'You'll have to wait four years to become a waiter.' I say, 'I'll wait.'"

Fred had been a professional busboy for a grand total of two months, but the Maitre d' hired him the next day. While working at The Plaza, Fred began to speak with George M. Cohan and his son, Junior.

As already discussed, the great entertainer continued to show up into the late 1930's, though he grew old, embittered and out of touch with the new Broadway. The son, though, never abandoned his friend Fred.

"Some years ago," Fred recollects, "he walked in those doors with his wife and I recognized him immediately. And I started calling him Junior! We had a ball, took pictures with the plaque." That was for the 50th Anniversary celebration.

In 1941, Fred officially became a waiter, wanting desperately to go after the Captain's position. The Captain is the Head Waiter's right hand man, and he, basically, takes care of the room and the rest of the waiting staff. But the war intervened and Fred enlisted, landing in Utah Beach with the Normandy Invasion. Finally, "in '58, I became a Captain." Next stop, wine steward for two years, donning the red jacket; then a manager and then, at long last, Maitre d'.

"I still have people I helped for years come in on Wednesday and Thursday to see me, and they say, 'Fred, when you're not here, it's not the same.'"

To say that would be an understatement. Without Fred the Oak Room would splinter apart. It's been that way for numerous years. Age shows no signs of stopping him, or even lessening his enthusiasm.

"I still feel like WOW!," he says.

Now, a few choice funny anecdotes from Fred:

"Oh. this is cute! I had a party of seven coming in one evening. Milton Berle, you know . . . great cigar smoker . . . he comes in and I always ask if there's something they'd like while waiting; make them comfortable. I said, 'Mr. Berle, what is your pleasure?' I never used that term before, how it came out I don't know. Man looks up at me with his cigar, rolling his rings (he loved rolling them), and says, 'Marilyn Monroe.' I looked at him and he was the cat that swallowed the canary . . . so satisfied about saying that. I'm looking back and I see Marilyn Monroe walks in! She sat at his table. He was the host, you see? So I got her a cocktail. What happened that night was they were both going to the circus and she was opening at Madison Square Garden that night riding a pink elephant."

Fred one time displayed some quick thinking when a bartender called him over and said not only was a customer refusing to pay his check but was threatening to shoot him. In a scene that could have come right out of the Old West, Fred said he called three security officers as backups and, "I put my hand in my tux jacket and said to the patron, 'You pull that gun and I'll kill you!' The guy turned around and said, 'You son of a bitch, you made me pay the check.' He was a retired cop but was bluffing about the gun. He had no gun!

"We used to put Cary Grant over there (pointing to an area blocked by a huge pillar; nobody could see the star), and nobody next to him, so he wouldn't be bothered. He always liked that table back there."

Other names dropped at the interview: Rod Steiger, Richard Chamberlain, Jason Robards, Humphrey Bogart, Rita Hayworth and so on. Fred's life can be considered that of a dream where everything that you ever wanted gets placed right in front of you — a bit like a Plaza menu.

Not that Fred hasn't come across his share of professional unpleasantries. Asked if he's had problems with rowdy drunks, he replies, "I used to cut them off if they had too much. I even cut off Conrad Hilton's lawyer. He had too much to drink. I walked him out the door nice and friendly, and I said, 'I'm concerned about you.' At the time, it was Hilton's hotel. I said, 'You are his attorney and I work for him.' And, he straightened out. It's the way you approach it. I had some lulus.

"One guy tried to walk out on me. I caught him in the revolving door, my foot in the door, had him like a canary. Made him come back and pay the tab. I was never reported or struck and had him pay the tip to the service staff."

By the year 2001, Fred was on duty one day a week, 4:00 P.M, to midnight, and stayed overnight at the hotel on the hotel. But even though he was technically only working one shift, he started working long before his actual shift was slated to begin and couldn't help coming to "check the room" the next morning.

He also still catered to the special needs of his longtime VIP guests such as former Secretary of State James Baker. "When he checks into the hotel, he calls about two months ahead of time, he says, 'Make sure Fred is there.' I gave him a vodka martini and then blue point oysters with shells still on top, like we used to do years ago. They're freshly opened but with the tops on. And then after that he has steak tartar, that's one of his favorites. I used to make steak tartar for the first lady of The Philippines, Imelda Marcos. She didn't live here. She stayed at the Waldorf. But she used to come to the Oak Room on the way to the opera. And Charlton Heston. And Leonard Bernstein when he came from the symphony. Steak tartar. Red meat. You've got to be a meat lover, though!"

While Fred and steak tartar have had a special allure for James Baker, Rex Harrison, Marcos and others, some like Al Pacino just like the old world grandeur of the Oak Room. Pacino and his gal pal Beverly D'Angelo surprised Fred when the couple was leaving the restaurant and D'Angelo turned to give Fred a tip. "No, no," Fred protested. "Mr. Pacino wants you to have it," insisted D'Angelo.

"You know what Donald Trump use to call me when he introduced me to people?" Fred proudly recalls. "'This is the First Sergeant of the Oak Room.' In other words, there are a lot of commanding officers here but this is The First Sergeant."

PLAZA PANACHE — JACK LEMMON IN THE EDWARDIAN ROOM, NOW ONE C.P.S.

THE BEATLES INVADE THE PLAZA AND AMERICA IN FEBRUARY 1964. THE YOUNG LADY IS THE DAUGHTER OF THE PHOTOGRAPHER. SHE RECOLLECTS THAT, "MY DAD CALLED ME AT SCHOOL AND SAID, 'COME DOWN HERE QUICKLY. I WANT YOU TO MEET THE BEATLES.'"

CAMELOT AT THE PLAZA: SENATOR J.F.K. AND JACKIE ATTEND A CHARITY SOIREE

JOAN CRAWFORD AND DEBONAIR ESCORT FRANCHOT TONE, WHEN NIGHTCLUBBING
WAS THE THING

JUDY GARLAND AND
ESCORT EARL
BLACKWELL ARRIVE FOR A
PLAZA
BLACK-TIE AFFAIR

MIA FARROW AND MOM MAUREEN O'SULLIVAN DINING IN THE EDWARDIAN ROOM

MILTON BERLE AND GRACE MARTIN CELEBRATE PLAZA STYLE

BOB AND DOLORES HOPE AND FRIEND — THE PLAZA HAS A HISTORY OF ACCOMMODATING GUESTS' PETS

MARILYN MONROE AT THE PLAZA PRESS EVENT FOR *THE PRINCE AND THE SHOWGIRL*

CARY GRANT HEADING *NORTH BY NORTHWEST* FROM 59TH STREET, ONE OF MANY PLAZA
LOCATION SHOOTS

WALTER MATTHAU AT THE FIFTH AVENUE ENTRANCE IN NEIL SIMON'S *PLAZA SUITE*

BEFORE JANE FONDA AND ROBERT REDFORD WENT *BAREFOOT IN THE PARK*, SHE WENT BAREFOOT IN A
PLAZA CORRIDOR

HOLLYWOOD MEETS
BROADWAY AT THE
PLAZA: MARY MARTIN
AND CHARLTON
HESTON

GLORIA SWANSON
READY FOR A CLOSE-
UP WITH ONE OF THE
PLAZA MAGNETA
CLOCKS, WHICH
ANNOYED ENRICO
CARUSO

KAY THOMPSON, BEFORE SHE CREATED ELOISE, WAS A TOP NIGHTCLUB PERFORMER. HERE SHE LAUGHS IT
UP WITH BACK-UP GROUP THE WILLIAMS BROTHERS, INCLUDING ANDY

THE INCOMPARABLE HILDEGARDE HELPED MAKE THE PERSIAN ROOM (SEEN HERE AFTER THE DIAMOND
PATTERN REDESIGN) LEGENDARY

KING HUSSEIN OF MOROCCO AND GRANDCHILDREN WITH FORMER PLAZA PRESIDENT
RICHARD WILHELM

FORMER PLAZA
MANAGER PHILIP
HUGHES
HOBNOBS
WITH ANGIE
DICKINSON

ONE-TIME QUEEN
OF THE PLAZA,
IVANA TRUMP,
WITH SINGER
WAYNE NEWTON

DONALD TRUMP NOT ONLY OWNED THE PLAZA, HE HELPED PROMOTE IT IN SUCH FILMS AS *HOME ALONE 2*.
HERE HE'S BEING COACHED BY THE FILM'S DIRECTOR, CHRIS COLUMBUS

SENATOR HILARY CLINTON GREETS THE PLAZA'S VICE PRESIDENT AND GENERAL MANAGER GARY
SCHWEIKERT, CENTER, AND DIRECTOR OF CATERING LAWRENCE HARVEY, RIGHT

HEAD PLAZA CHEF
BRUNO TISON
OVERSEES THE HOTEL'S
MANY,
AND VARIED,
RESTAURANTS — BUT
STILL NO COFFEE
SHOP

CHAIRMAN KWEK LENG BENG, OF SINGAPORE, IS THE NEW CO-OWNER OF THE PLAZA

THE OTHER NEW CO-OWNER IS PRINCE ALWALEED BIN TALAL OF SAUDI ARABIA

MORE ROYALTY AT THE PLAZA — DUKE ELLINGTON IN THE GRAND BALLROOM

※

Speaking of whom . . . Once upon a time, The Donald made his queen Ivana president of The Plaza and its working chief operations officer. This meant someone had to be brought in to do the actual job.

First it was Richard Wilhelm, an all-around hotel man with a gift for picking the best people. Then it was Barry Cregan, touted as "a numbers man" by Donald Trump, and one of the industry's heavy-duty workaholics by others. He was brought in to take up where Wilhelm left off in late 1992. Cregan didn't seem to mind the fourteen hours or more he had to put in both running and toeing the bankers' line each day.

He also graciously touched upon a touchy subject during our interview, hotel security:

"When you walk in here you always wonder is there too much or too little security. But recent events have maybe changed one's view on that. When the Trade Center blew up, Per (Hellman) at the Waldorf and I were on the phone the next day because there are two hotels that could be a target. We have good security. We don't have a garage and after the World Trade Center, it made us think that maybe we were better off without it. The caliber of customers we have on a constant basis probably puts us in the spotlight, but it also protects us from it. Meaning that we do so much diplomacy business here that we are in constant communication with the agencies and the Secret Service and the FBI. We constantly have them around us and we interact with them, and consequently I think it's a safer place.

"If you look at our security, it is more modeled after the secret service. We don't use the walkie-talkies in a visible way. Instead we use the ear plug and the wrist thing. At times I think people probably think it is the Secret Service rather than an in-house security function."

(Which reminds me of Vito down in the subbasement, who told me a story of how he got a call from a guy — he gets all

these wild requests — who says "come and screw my leg in."
He didn't know what the guy was talking about. Was it a job
for security? Or maybe the Vice Squad? Nope. Literally, that's
what it was. The guy needed help screwing his false leg in. And
so Vito helped him.)

I asked Cregan about another delicate area, customer complaints.

"A lady called me once. She was here during the blizzard.
She had on white pants. 'They stained my pants,' she said. We
also know she was walking around during the snowstorm getting them dirty. I said, 'What's the value of them?' She said,
'$125.' I said, 'You got it.'"

※

Blame it on the uniform.

As a corporal in the Army in the South Pacific before being
a part of the Army occupation of Japan for eight months under
General Douglas MacArthur after World War II, Joe Szorentini
had seen plenty of men in uniform festooned with all kinds of
stripes and medals. But it wasn't until one bright sunny day
as he was walking along 59th Street, shortly after he got out of
his Army outfit, did he see a Plaza doorman in a uniform Joe
wanted to wear for the rest of his life — or at least the next 53
years of it.

"He had such a beautiful uniform," Joe recollects. His next
thought was, "I think I'll be a doorman. I knew right off the bat
I'd be happy — it's such a prestigious hotel. I'd always read
about the people who came here."

On Joe's very first day on the door, January 16, 1947, after
several months as an elevator operator, he met Charlie
Chaplin. Then, a day later, the diminutive Edward G.
Robinson, who "collected" hotels (he loved to live lavishly in
some of the best suites of New York hotels).

"My very first day at The Plaza I was on the service car elevator in the 'back of the house' with all the freight and all the
food," Joe relates. "This was on the 58th Street side of The

Plaza. Then I moved over to the elevators on the 59th Street side. You see, on the service elevator, you didn't need a uniform. I worked in my street clothes. When you moved over to the 59th Street side the fun of it was you got a beautiful uniform. And then I moved to the door two years later in 1949."

"I loved it," he exclaims. "It never changed."

Over the years, The Plaza has taken very seriously the designing of its employee uniforms from the gilt-braided doormen to the housekeepers and handymen and at times has even called upon some of the best and brightest names in the fashion world to create exactly the right look. Famed fashion and stage designer Donald Brooks proclaimed, for example, of his Plaza "line" that, "There are fifty-five categories of uniforms in all . . . and The Plaza personnel will not resemble a group of ancient circus ringmasters. The uniforms, instead, will be suitable, functional and comfortable."

As a doorman, Joe says he "would come in at 7 A.M. and work until 3:30 P.M. one week on 59th Street and the following week on Fifth Avenue. Then I became a relief man. The 7 to 3:30 man would be there. I'd come in at 10 o'clock in the morning and give him a half hour and then he'd come back and I'd go around to the Fifth Avenue side and give him a half hour relief. And that was five days a week. After the morning break I'd come back and give him a half hour at lunch and then go to the other door and give him a half hour. That way I worked both doors in one day. I got to see everybody."

"I tried to be humble and polite to everybody, no matter how big or small they were," Joe told friends and family and members of the media who gathered January 18, 2000 to pay him some long overdue respects at his retirement party, complete with a huge cake in the shape of the grand hotel.

But when an English singing group and several thousand of their fans descended on the hotel in 1964, Joe says he really didn't know they were anything that special.

"I unloaded the luggage from the Beatles limo," he said. "But I just thought they were another one of those English singing groups. I was surprised when they went on *The Ed Sullivan Show* and were so good!"

Joe fondly remembers that in the late 1940's Frank Sinatra, before he rented a permanent suite at the Waldorf Towers of The Waldorf-Astoria Hotel, stayed at The Plaza from time to time when he was in New York. (One of those times, popular legend has it, the Chairman of the Board chased Lana Turner — the so-called Hollywood "sweater girl" — up and down the sixth floor of the hotel. They weren't exactly having a fight. The report goes that they were "frolicking." No one is sure if they had their clothes on or not. Maybe they were in those gorgeous Plaza robes the hotel provides to all guests.)

Joe also remembers Marilyn Monroe coming into the hotel during the 50's but not staying overnight. "She used to come in and have lunch or dinner at the Edwardian Room."

Of Audrey Hepburn, Joe remembers, "an angel. She talked so beautiful and she treated me like I was somebody.

"Peter Bogdonovich, he stayed there quite a lot. The last time I saw him was over a year ago. He looked the same — maybe a little grayer."

"Your dad, Ward," Joe adds on a personal note, "used to give me a dollar or two every time I got a cab for him. That was a lot of money in those days." Of course, Jackie Gleason used to give Joe $50 every time he got him a cab, and Sinatra would slip him $20, although Joe said, "very often he'd give it to one of the men who was with him, like his driver, and he would give it to me. A couple of times he gave it to me directly."

Speaking of the differences at The Plaza when he first started to work there and more recent years, the most noticeable change, he feels, is the way people dress. "At The Plaza you were dressed up in the old days."

Joe recalls Barbra Streisand was forever, in those pre-cellular phone days, looking for a phone. Barbra stayed at The Plaza for a week while she was filming the Ray Stark-Sydney Pollack movie *The Way We Were*, written by Arthur Laurents, co-starring Robert Redford, in 1973. "All the shooting at The Plaza was outside by the Fifth Avenue entrance, but nearer 58th Street. . . I got along good with her. She's changed. But she always used to ask me, 'Where's that phone again? That phone.' You know, the Fifth Avenue house phone in the box on the right hand side of the front entrance booth. It seems she was always calling someone. The phone's still there. They rebuilt it and it's a big thing now. It was an old little tiny box years ago. If you're a guest in the hotel you can get an outside line but nobody else can."

About Cary Grant, who was in *North by Northwest*, partially filmed at The Plaza, Joe said, "Oh, a real nice guy. He stayed there while he was doing the movie. He was there for about a week."

Although Grant had the reputation of being very watchful of his money, Joe says he was a "pretty good tipper," usually doling out at least a dollar for a cab. But the greatest tipper of all had to be Jackie Gleason, Joe reiterates in awe.

One of the biggest changes Joe's seen at The Plaza over his many years is the almost total absence of permanent guests now.

In fact, Plaza insiders say the very last longtime permanent guest left the hotel in the mid-1990's. At the time, this lady had been paying comparatively little rent. She'd been there so long her rent increases fell under the rent-control restrictions.

And did Joe ever stay at the hotel he so zealously guarded?

"Once, on our 25th anniversary," Joe's bride, Veronica, fondly interjects.

While some employees use The Plaza as a springboard to other careers, others like Scott Griffith, director of housekeeping, may have found their career home.

One of the top several dozen executives at The Plaza, Scott's goal is to be director of rooms, which is one step above his own as director of housekeeping.

A native of Cincinnati, Scott "started off at Marriott Hotels.

I worked in housekeeping in many small hotels and I wanted to come to the city and I was walking through the doors of The Waldorf-Astoria and said to myself, 'My gosh, they're never going to hire me. I'll never get the opportunity to work here and I proceeded to work my way up and I was the only assistant director of housekeeping to ever be promoted to director of housekeeping."

As the head of a small army of more than 200 people, he manages room attendants, housemen, maids, porters, bathroom attendants, "PM ladies" (bed turndown room attendants), window washers, shampoo men, marble cleaners, to name just a few.

"I have 111 AM room attendants, 35 PM room attendants," he said. "I had 400 on staff at the Waldorf."

He's also in charge of fixing chairs and sofas. The upholstery department is on the 18th floor in an unrenovated room overlooking Central Park. "I'd switch with them any day. We used to do all the shade and lace repair downstairs and that's all been relocated and combined with the upholstery shop now."

His responsibilities overlap with the security department. "One of my PM runners [who take odds and ends such as toothbrushes to guests], noticed this guy in the back of the house area and he went out of his way to make sure he reported it. Stayed by. Watched him. Called security. Everything he was supposed to do to make sure nothing happened to any of our guests or our colleagues."

While security at The Plaza is extremely tight, when it is breached, as with someone wondering in the halls who is not a guest, staff is quick to respond.

Juggling rooms for VIPs can be a hair-raising business at times when not the least expensive but most expensive suites are sought after. When Queen Noor of Jordan decided to stay at The Plaza at the last minute Halloween night, 2000, it seemed little The Plaza could do to accommodate her in the manner to which she was accustomed. By convincing several other guests to move to other suites, Queen Noor and her family were able to get a premier suite facing Central Park.

Parting Thoughts

Devotees of The Plaza share a sense of personal ownership with the hotel. It's as much "their" hotel as it is
"their" apartment or "their" car. It's an emotional tie that
crosses all economic segments of society, affecting the rich,
"who are different from you and me," as Scott Fitzgerald told
us, no more than the middle income couple in for their
anniversary.

So I thought I would close with memories of The Plaza by a
broad array of folk, from movie stars to Broadway producers to
writers and lesser known people.

"Once you come through the great doors of The Plaza, everybody automatically, no matter what walk of life they are from
— whether it's a tourist walking through to see the famous
Plaza Hotel, a top corporate officer staying here in a suite for a
few nights — all of a sudden they take on a feeling of civility,"
states Richard Wilhelm, the former manager of The Plaza in the
1980s and early 1990s. "Everyone walks into this red-carpet-
ed marble environment and immediately it's like walking into
a great museum. It's really a refined environment and they
take on that character."

For film star Michael York, his favorite thing at The Plaza Hotel is "tea at the Palm Court. I think tea is a wonderful institution. Because it comes at a time of day when you need a little buildup."

David G. Koebs of Davies, Florida, won a $10 million Publishers Clearing House Award and a trip to New York which included a stay at The Plaza. "I was afraid to sit on the commode because it was made of gold," he told reporters afterward.

Martin Riskin, who worked in both the banquet departments of The Plaza and the Waldorf, says the "most beautiful occasions I've had the pleasure of working on at The Plaza are the golden wedding anniversaries, where you'd see a couple who had been married for 50 years, their children and their grandchildren all together."

Martin Kaufman, who co-produced the Broadway musical *Grand Hotel*, stayed at The Plaza for two weeks after his shower door shattered in his apartment on Central Park South, the same Art Deco apartment building, as a matter of fact, that actress Sylvia Miles lives in. He escaped with some minor scratches but the experience shook him up. "So I figured I wanted to stay in one of the nicest hotels on Central Park South. This was in 1984 or '85 or so. I tried the Essex House and it was booked. And I got to the end of the block and there was only The Plaza left. They didn't have a regular room. But I begged them and I actually got a room there, an inside room and it was lovely. Tiny but lovely. A bathroom with a vaulted ceiling. I actually got a room at The Plaza for $120 a night and I said to myself, 'This is cheaper than staying at home'. I stayed there two weeks. I couldn't believe I could stay at The Plaza that cheap."

"I lived at The Plaza from the time I was born until I was

three and a half," remembers Lois Womer, who resided there with her parents. (She swears she never poured water down the mail chutes.) Her father was the late magazine publisher Eltinge Warner, who published *The Smart Set, Field and Stream*, and many other magazines.

"I remember that Paul was the head waiter of a dining room that eventually became the Persian Room," says Womer, who still lives in New York City. "We tea-danced in this room in the afternoon and it was wonderful. And then at night it became a dinner and supper club.

"I remember my baby carriage, which had a hood made of beaver to keep me warm, was kept at the 58th Street entrance to the hotel. I don't know if that side entrance still exists. (It does but it's often closed for security reasons.) But my carriage sat there. We had a suite and I had a baby nurse who pushed me around Central Park. When I was three and a half we moved up to 1088 Park Avenue which I hated. My parents had a duplex penthouse there and I hated that. I hated being 'up there.' I liked being right on the park.

"I went to dancing class at The Plaza — Miss Robinson's dancing class in the grand ballroom, every Wednesday afternoon. I carried my dancing shoes — patent leather, of course, in a little leather bag and you changed your shoes when you got there and there was Miss Robinson and her two assistants. And we — it was all girls — learned to fox-trot and to tango, etc. going around and around that ballroom. I was seven years old or so. Years later, I remember going tea dancing at The Plaza. You'd have one Brandy Alexander and get up and dance madly around the room."

For singer Rosemary Clooney, The Plaza will always be a beautiful missed opportunity. Although she wanted to sing at The Plaza's Persian Room she never got the chance. But, she told me, "I used to stay at The Plaza all the time. I'll never forget the time we had seven rooms on one floor and a Christmas tree from FAO Schwartz, a live tree that they had decorated. It was one of the nicest Christmases I ever had. A real tree that they themselves came over and decorated and did it all."

⌗

Finally, there are my own treasured recollections.

Aside from lighting gunpowder with my father in the kitchen sink of his sixth-floor suite, I have other peronal memories of The Plaza. My stepmother invited me to the hotel to see Lainie Kazan sing and I immediately fell in love with her. Ironically, however, with all the celebrities I've interviewed over the years, including Robert Goulet, who sang at the Persian Room, I never ran into Kazan again. I do remember hearing that she was singing at this or that nightclub not too long ago and told John Springer, the publicist handling her, that "She's gorgeous." And I was somewhat surprised when John, who was always diplomatic, shot back, "She was gorgeous, all right" and then it dawned on me that it was more than 25 years since I had seen her sing at The Plaza and my impression of her today was still colored by that first glimpse.

After I went to the American Academy of Dramatic Art to study acting and got my first job at the American Shakespeare Festival in Stratford, Connecticut, I succeeded in convincing a young lady who worked in the concession stand to join me on a Saturday I had off for a day of lunch and the Broadway theater in New York. Well, I got tickets to *The Royal Hunt of The Sun* and even though I was the son of a well known drama critic who could have gotten free seats I paid for my seats and proceeded to entertain my date royally. But if I had paid for our lavish lunch at The Plaza's Trader Vic's, which included several exotic "fruit drinks" spiked with alcohol, I would have had nothing left over to get my date back to Stratford by taxi and train. So, having one of my father's business cards, I boldly "signed" for the lunch by signing one of these cards. It was immediately accepted by the manager as my father was a frequent guest at the restaurant. The bill came to close to $100 and when my father opened a letter from Trader Vic's with my "charge" he let out a scream that could be heard on 42nd Street and he was living up on East 71st Street at the time. He called my mother and I paid my father back out of my savings from my $55 a week job in the Shakespeare company. Meanwhile, I had kissed my date goodnight — in a very gentile fashion, fitting the unaffordable extravagance of the moment — and never saw her again. Was it worth it? Well, it was a sort of roundabout way of introducing me to the life of a newspaperman which is fueled partly by invitations to glamorous restaurants and shows as well as the chance to meet and write about interesting and exciting people.

Sometimes these days, as I walk or drive by the grand hotel on the southern tip of Central Park, I sometimes picture a wide-eyed little boy enjoying the wonder of it all and that little boy is me.

It's thirty-odd years ago now since I first started wondering about what was going on behind those big, double-doored suites as I scurried on to my father's own Plaza residence. I know I haven't found out all the answers, all the secrets. But one never wants a beautiful mystery completely exposed.

The Plaza is as much a lovely state of mind as it is a beautiful building. No matter where I am, no matter how troubled a day it may have been, a certain content wells up inside me whenever I hark back to the good times that have taken place for me and for thousands, maybe millions, of other privileged guests at this uniquely remarkable corner of the globe.

I hope I've opened a few doors for you, too.

THE PLAZA BUSINESS: PART II

The Prince, The Chairman, and The Future

G rand hotels are born of time and circumstance and great minds and great wealth. But they become great when they're owned and managed to perfection as The Plaza is now. In December 1994, I broke the story for the New York *Post* that there was an interested buyer for The Plaza. And, indeed, while that party had made a bid, a deal to purchase the Grande Dame was struck between Kwek Leng Beng, Chairman of the Hong Leong Group, parent of CDL Hotels and Prince Alwaleed Bin Talal of Saudi Arabia.

"Perhaps the main problem for The Plaza over the years has been the difference of opinion between management and ownership. And in many cases the priorities have been often reversed. The managements have been more concerned with maintaining the asset and the owners with the promotion side [to make more of a profit]," said Paul Underhill, The Plaza's asset manager. As such, Underhill represents the interests of The Plaza's two owners, Chairman Kwek and Prince Alwaleed.

"We're fortunate to have assembled a group of owners with the flare of Mr. Trump, the business acumen of Prince Alwaleed and Chairman Kwek, a devoted owner of hotels, to further enhance The Plaza as one of the premier hotels of the world today," continued Underhill.

Still, The Plaza ownership change was something of a happy accident. Chairman Kwek and Hong Leong, which already owned and/or operated 35 hotels in 1995, didn't actively pursue acquisition of The Plaza.

Chairman Kwek had already purchased the Millenium (this millennium, called the Millenium Hilton, is spelled with just one "N") in the Wall Street area and told me, in an exclusive interview at the Millennium Mayfair in London, "I thought it was useful to have the Millennium Broadway and little did I know at the time I would also buy The Plaza.

"And all of a sudden, one of my principle bankers at Citibank approached me and asked us to take a look at The Plaza. I didn't know it would ever be sold, especially with all the publicity which said it was a 'trophy hotel.' But I decided to take a look at it. It is a beautiful building. But more than that, The Plaza is about location, location, location. It had the potential of generating large profits, with more than 800 rooms.

"So we started to have a dialogue with Citibank and then we got exclusivity," he continued. "A week later, Shaukat Aziz, the Finance Minister of Pakistan (who was then with Citibank Singapore as one of two regional heads and in charge of global finance for the Asia-Pacific), whom I had known for a great many years, approached me and said, 'Have you heard of Prince Alwaleed?' I said, 'Yes, but I have not kept up-to-date with what he's been doing.'

"Shaukat said the prince — who would be my good strategic partner as both of us were on the same wavelength when it came to business — would like to form a joint venture with me on The Plaza. I said 'It's a great honor to be partnering with the prince.'

"We were supposed to meet in London. But at the last minute the prince was unable to come, so he sent his private jet to pick me up from London to Riyadh. It was my first time in Riyadh. I believe the plane was a Boeing 727 specially converted for His Highness. The interior is impressive — with a gold-plated toilet, one master bedroom, a sitting room and two stewards in attendance. I was put up at a suite at The Inter-Continental and the next day I was driven to his palace for a meeting at around 11 A.M. And there we met for the first time and had a wonderful discussion. The meeting took place with his whole entourage waiting in attendance at the far end of the enormous sitting room and the prince and me conversing privately at the other end. During the meeting, the prince and I agreed that The Plaza was an outstanding hotel. The hotel was a little run down as previous owners had not done full restorative work on the property. The prince and I therefore agreed that we would restore the hotel to its former glory. It was a good meeting. I was impressed with how active the prince was.

"We also exchanged views about the hotel industry, particularly in the U.S. We shared the same view that the U.S. economy was going to do well over the next few years and in particular the hotel industry would be performing strongly as the year progressed. Much as we would have liked to buy the hotel for a much cheaper price, the fact remained that this was a trophy hotel, for which we had negotiated for a minimum price [reportedly, $325]. But we were confident that the hotel would perform. Besides the risks would be spread with a joint venture partner. That was in April, 1995.

At first glance, Mr. Kwek Leng Beng, the chairman of the Hong Leong Group in the thriving city-state of Singapore, may have seemed an unlikely buyer of The Plaza, even in his own mind, but not since legendary hotelier Conrad Hilton bought The Plaza a half century earlier has the hotel had such a knowledgeable and resourceful hotelman at the helm. Together with Prince Alwaleed, who is one of the world's most astute businessmen and long-term investors, their stewardship of this most unique landmark is par excellence.

The number of hotels owned and mostly operated by Hong Leong Group's Millennium and Copthorne hotel division has grown from 35 in 1995 to more than 100 today. These include some other famous trophy properties such as The Biltmore in Los Angeles and The Knickerbocker in Chicago.

Articulate, polite and imbued with a sense of humor, a quality shared by Conrad Hilton, Chairman Kwek says he has big plans for The Plaza, which include eventually adding those three floors of suites on top of the hotel. He has been careful to husband its record profit growth to help put it on the best fiscal as well as physical footing its been on in years. In the process, he's winning plaudits from the press and preservationists alike. In the December 2000 edition of *Management Today*, the Millennium and Copthorne Hotels were ranked 59th of 248 "most admired" companies in Great Britain in terms of management, assets and profits. In the hotel and leisure class alone, M&C was ranked number three, ahead of fourth-ranked Hilton.

Chairman Kwek's "headline-grabbing bid for The Plaza Hotel in New York won him international attention," Ed Paisley wrote in *Institutional Investor*. Paisley quoted Chairman Kwek as saying, "Financing hotel acquisitions is the easy part, management is the hard part."

"We did what we could to restore the hotel to its original condition as fast as possible," Chairman Kwek continued in his interview with me. "The decoration should fit the period of The Plaza. I love the architecture of The Plaza."

Personally, The Plaza has provided prestige for the international businessman in return for the firm financial footing he has given The Plaza. And while Chairman Kwek's company keeps the management on its toes and does not manage it on a day-to-day basis, Chairman Kwek will "sometimes call the manager and ask what the occupancy rate is."

"If a manager doesn't know this [and Plaza mangers have never been known not to know this] he's not on the ball. It's the most basic thing . . . Once in a while I check it. We have board meetings.

"Don't forget our role is to 'asset manage' not manage. But a good manager of a hotel is essential to increase profitably."

As to profits at The Plaza, "profits have gone up [in recent years] thanks to the brand name 'The Plaza' and thanks to all the refurbishment we've done," he said. "All rooms have been refurbished and there is a new restaurant at the Edwardian Room [One C.P.S.]."

In fact, at the time of the news (in 1995) that apartments might be built atop The Plaza, Chairman Kwek received more than fifteen offers to buy the suites once they are built regardless of price. But, like his partner the prince, Chairman Kwek wants to avoid even the appearance of disrupting guests at a time when occupancy is improving and more basic restoration steps are being completed as priority.

Inevitably, "some people may be inconvenienced by the construction on the roof and the necessary scaffolding and crane," Chairman Kwek concedes.

If it were left to him entirely, Chairman Kwek said he would make The Plaza "a six-star hotel. Our first objective is to maintain profitability. And you mustn't be afraid of charging the right price."

The chairman, who spends two-thirds of the year in Singapore and one-third globe-trotting to various world capitals where he has holdings, was born and raised in Singapore.

"My father, came from China originally. He started as a building supplier and then he went into real estate. Not as a developer. Subsequently he got into development. His first love was real estate and, of course, I learned a lot from him. I took over the chairmanship of Hong Leong Group in 1990, although I had been actively leading several companies within the group well before that."

It was Chairman Kwek who got the Hong Leong Group into the hotel business in a big way, based on the chairman's strong conviction that because "the hotel business is an international business" it would have a globalizing influence on the rest of the company. Also, growing affluence and the increasingly competitive airfares augur well for the hotel industry. "You buy a hotel with your knowledge of real estate, add value to the property and then you sell it at the right time for a good hefty profit. That's the objective I originally had in mind. But I have learned if you have good assets and create a brand then you must be reckoned with. A lot of people believe that at the end of the day sheer size is the key to survival. But The Savoy in London can stand alone. And other hotels can stand alone in a particular niche and I strongly believe, with good management, The Plaza can stand alone even though it doesn't have to."

At the time I talked with him, Chairman Kwek said he had no specific plans to buy additional properties in the U.S. market. "I have a policy that you cannot pinpoint acquisitions and say, in effect, 'Next year I'm going to acquire ten hotels' because the conditions may not be conducive. Also, opportunities may not come knocking at your door. Conversely, when the golden opportunity does knock at your door, you have to seize it."

According to the *Forbes* magazine 15th annual list of the world's richest people, Alsaud, Prince Alwaleed Bin Talal, 44, a nephew of King Fahd of Saudi Arabia, is the sixth best off with a net worth of $20 billion. (Bill Gates leads the list with $60 billion, followed by three other Americans, including Warren Buffett, and then a German family, Theo and Karl Albrecht.) The Prince, who is married with two children, is based in the royal palace in Riyadh, Saudi Arabia, and his $9.6 billion stake in Citigroup is his largest holding. For fun, he told me "he relaxes in Europe" and, according to *Forbes*, he "takes long walks near his weekend desert retreat."

In January 2001, Chairman Kwek and HRH Prince Alwaleed bought out the remaining 12 percent of The Plaza that Citibank had owned, Chairman Kwek told me. "At the time of purchase [in 1995], the prince and CDL Hotels were negotiating for a 50 percent stake each in the ownership of The Plaza Hotel. However, both parties managed to secure only 41.6 percent each with the banks holding the balance. It was agreed with the banks that should they wish to sell their stake the prince and CDL Hotels have the right of first refusal. The prince and CDL Hotels now own 50 percent each in The Plaza Hotel."

I interviewed Prince Alwaleed personally in early April 2000, and found him to be not only articulate but someone with unabashed affection for The Plaza. He also lavished praise on his partner and co-owner of The Plaza, Chairman Kwek, with whom, he revealed, he is very comfortable co-overseeing the management of The Plaza.

"Mr. Kwek is an incredible partner and I like him a lot. I leave in his hands completely the management of The Plaza," the prince explained.

"In the whole world, I believe, as far as the hotel business is concerned, there are several icons. For example, in the United States, on the East coast there's The Plaza and on the West coast there's the Fairmont in San Francisco. If you go to the Far East another icon is The Regent in Hong Kong and in France another icon is The George V and all these hotels I'm involved with them. So really to me to be involved with The Plaza is something very important to me . . . as our policy is to have special icons whenever we are involved in this industry."

Do you enjoy staying at The Plaza when you're in New York?

"Yes, I always stay at The Plaza when I'm in New York. In New York, I have this hotel. I have the Four Seasons and I also have the Pierre Hotel which is managed by Four Seasons [management company]. But I always stay at The Plaza."

Asked if he brings his own chef with him he emphatically said, "Oh, no, no, no. We will use the food The Plaza has. I use a big area of the Palm Court as my office. We always do our transactions there. All my business is conducted there."

Is he still as optimistic about the U.S. economy and The Plaza's future profits?

"There is no doubt the U.S. economy is experiencing a slowdown, which hopefully will not turn into a recession. But you know there have been nearly ten years of incredible growth and inevitably you'll have some slowdown. And a slowdown really would be healthy to cut down on all the excesses that took place in many industries. But as far as The Plaza is concerned we're not experiencing any slowdown at all at this stage."

Will you and the chairman eventually move forward on the plan to build suites on the roof of The Plaza?

"The project was put on hold and we did not want to do too much because we spent so much to get the hotel back in shape and right now we're enjoying a big momentum and we don't want to disturb that momentum by having new construction at The Plaza Hotel."

His favorite of his hotels?

"These are very unusual properties. You can't really compare them. Each one is its own icon in its own place. The Plaza, the George V, the Regent Hotel. These are incredible icons that are never going to be repeated again."

"When Prince Alwaleed comes in it's all hands on deck so to speak," explains Jeffrey Jacobs, The Plaza's director of food and beverage. "He's very respectful of our employees and they like him. He wants to own the best things in the world, including the best hotels. And to him this is the best location and certainly one of the best hotels in New York. He has the George V in Paris . . . we need people like that who are the keepers of the treasures of the world. . . . He really believes in luxury. He doesn't want to develop chain hotels. It's not just about making money; it's about making money on certain levels. He buys things that he really believes in. He has a firm belief in what his companies are doing. It's about aligning his businesses with the way he lives. That's really great because the Fairmont hotels and The Plaza are really aligned with his philosophy of quality and what things should be. So when he decides to put money into this hotel and invest and decides he wants to build suites on the 18th floor or a spa you never say to him, 'At what level do you want to do it?' You know that he only wants the best."

Speaking of, and for, Fairmont, Bill Fatt, Chairman and C.E.O of Fairmont Hotels & Resorts told me, "The Plaza, with its illustrious history and preeminent market position is one of the most celebrated hotels in the world. Capturing the essence of Fairmont, this remarkable icon embodies the spirit, depth and grace of our storied collection. The Plaza offers the best address in New York and is often seen as the pulse of its community. With other legendary hotels such as The Fairmont Banff Springs, The Fairmont Scottsdale Princess and The Fairmont San Francisco in our portfolio, The Plaza helps position North America's largest luxury brand on the world stage."

And "the most exciting part of The Plaza is now coming. The team has all been put together. It's perfect. And probably for the whole period since the 1940s The Plaza has never had this opportunity," Underhill said.

"This is a unique moment in time for the hotel," agrees Gary Schweikert, vice-president and general manager. "I've been lucky enough to stay in the New York area where my family is located, having worked at the Waldorf, and I thought that was such a magical place and having the honor to be here as well it's hard to imagine what comes next. Our business is similar to the theater. It's setting the stage for people. The people we want to be on stage are the customers and the grand old hotel.

"The current ownership is so supportive of everything we're trying to do. They really see the potential of this hotel. There's a very strong, heartfelt desire to make it one of the very best hotels in New York City, the country and even the world. Their intentions are so fantastically oriented toward betterment of the hotel that it's extraordinary. Because they have a long term vision; it's not just about the year 2002 or the year 1995 when they first became involved. It's really about where The Plaza is going to be in the next ten to twenty years and what can we do to make our mark here.

"The hotel really deserves it. It's the icon of hotels in the industry. All around the world it's always recognized. It's also one of the icon buildings in New York City. No picture book of New York is complete without it. Our endorsements and third-party strategic alliances are very strong and of very, very high quality. And I think the ownership recognizes all that so I think we're at a moment in time where we can say there's so much that can be done here. We have a supportive ownership, a strong economy, so we've really dedicated ourselves both from the guest services point of view and toward physical plant improvement because we feel the hotel really deserves it. It needs to be on top.

"There has been a significant increase in the hotel's profitability in the 1990s but this was accomplished without negatively impacting guest services. We are very efficient operators but at the same time we still deliver the expectation; we still fulfill the dreams of people who want to stay at The Plaza. We want to make sure it's everything they expect it to be and everything it could possibly be but at the same time run it as an efficient business."

Tom Civitano, Underhill believes, has played a major role in "building for the future" because he "realizes that tradition is the key."

And Civitano, characteristically modest about tooting his own horn, is as bullish about The Plaza as George Steinbrenner, owner of the New York Yankees, is about The Yankees.

"Over the decade of the 90's the profit of The Plaza is considerably greater of what it had been in the 1980's," Civitano explains.

"One of the most satisfying results from a sales and marketing perspective over the years is that we have successfully continued to build upon the worldwide recognition of The Plaza while simultaneously it has also been a very profitable time, regardless of what the external factors may have been.

"That's one of the real brand strengths of The Plaza. Because of the tradition of excellence and all the notable guests that tradition has brought to us over the hundred years, people still want to see The Plaza and want to stay here. They've either seen it, heard about it or read about it. In each of the different decades, each one built on the previous one and the next one built upon that one, always the barometer for which others will be judged against — almost like The New York Yankees.

"When the Yankees won their most recent World Championship, it was not only that championship that was discussed, but that it was their 26th World Championship. People go to see the Yankees because of what they represent in baseball. And people visit The Plaza because of what it represents to New York and what it represents to the hotel business. And I think there are similarities there between the Yankees and The Plaza, which in itself is its own destination, and also happens to be in New York City."

"There are a number of things we have going to insure the long-term success of this building. You could certainly renovate every year if you had to but that doesn't make hotels great. That makes a new one. Our investment on the service side is equally as strong as it is on the product side," says Gary Schweikert. "We're constantly meeting with the staff and retraining and focusing on a very personalized level of service. Our main goal is to participate and predict what the customer wants. So they don't have to ask for it. To do that you have to have a very strong, almost intimate relationship with your customers to know what they're asking for; what their expectations are and then we have to train for that. So that's as big a focus as any.

"We have a fantastic collection of tenured employees, some

of whom have been with us twenty, thirty, forty years, and it's been a wonderful treat seeing these professionals in our industry impart their knowledge about the grand traditions of hospitality to the younger folks coming on board. That's a wonderful thing that our staff is great about. It's part of The Plaza's building for the future, trying even more to instill in its employees a greater sense of belonging to The Plaza family."

Because the management buck stops at Schweikert's second-floor office, he's had experience with customer complaints. A direct and outgoing man, Scheweikert doesn't hesitate to assume blame when the hotel has fallen short of someone's expectations.

But, he stresses, "You get to the point where, when you're having a difficult conversation with someone, you can only apologize so many times. If someone's upset with you it's because you didn't live up to their expectations, so the best you can do is to invite them back and promise to do it right. But most people I've dealt with are reasonable. What it's really about is getting the chance to rebuild people's confidence in you. If the good intentions are there on behalf of the hotel to make a bad situation right people are understanding. It's a people business.

"In our business you seek information from so many different sources," he adds. "We keep an eye not only on what our markets are doing but what our customers within our markets are doing. We look at the trade magazines, the business magazines such as *Forbes* to follow trends. And you look at what your competition is doing also. Certainly, I sit down and ask where are we now, where are we going for the rest of the year? What's changing. And certainly, on a yearly basis, we set aside a few days for the whole team to really brainstorm and ask, 'Are we doing the right thing and what can we do better?'

"We've done a very good job of marketing to the various segments of our customer base and that is clearly 70 percent business traveler during the week and for them we know we have to deliver a certain type of service. Everything from high technology, high-speed internet access in all the rooms to fax machines in all the rooms. Two-line phones, voice mail — all the things that a business person needs on the road today to be efficient. And from there we go on to the high-end leisure traveler on the weekend, who has a whole different set of expectations. Take care of my kids. Take care of my pets. What am I gong to get to see in New York? And for them it's fantasy land. So we deliver quite adequately to both sets of customers."

The Plaza is a multiple recipient of *Business Traveler* magazine's top honor as the best business hotel in North America, and the World Travel Awards' World's Leading Hotel for the last five years. Soon (if it doesn't already) the hotel will offer every person checking into the hotel the option of getting a free temporary cell phone which automatically rings when they're out of their room so no important business calls will be missed or delayed.

In January, 2000, an 8000-square-foot spa, complete with Roman columns, marble mosaic floors, wood basins with cut crystal sinks, opened at The Plaza.

"It's only fitting that one of the world's most elegant hotels has a spa whose wide range of services meet the needs of its sophisticated, international clientele," says Schweikert. "From the plush amenities such as Frette Robes in our treatment rooms to our innovative health and beauty treatments, The Plaza Spa is sure to become a destination for Plaza guests, Manhattan residents, day visitors and anyone in search of a true luxury spa experience."

Designed by SoHo-based architects Stonehill & Taylor, The Plaza Spa has private dressing rooms, steam and sauna rooms, as well as an "outdoor" atrium-like whirlpool bath. A workout called "business express" includes a "walk in the park," during which a personal trainer takes you through a workout in Central Park.

Aside from plans to rebuild and renovate the suites on the

hotel's 17th floor, work has already begun to apply a *trompe l'oiel* motif to the interior courtyard of The Plaza. Also, as mentioned, some thought has been given to replacing the roof of the Palm Court restaurant with glass, much like it originally was before that poor soul plunged through the original.

Besides its "Young Ambassadors" program, which provides VIP treatment at various New York tourist attractions to children of families staying at The Plaza, the hotel plans an ambitious building program of renovating suites on its 17th and 18th floors. The Plaza is also looking forward by looking back. As a component of its corporate marketing program, Fairmont Hotels & Resorts has established a heritage marketing program to provide guests at The Plaza and other of its hotels — from the Royal York in Toronto to the Hamilton Princess in Bermuda — with some of the hotels' most colorful and interesting histories. "As part of our program over the next year, we will be focusing on organizing the archival materials and having images [photos] scanned so that they can be made available," said Nancy Battet, Fairmont's heritage marketing manager.

Great landmarks don't, after all, survive on sheer good will. They require careful, even resourceful nurturing. The Plaza has come a long way since it rose in all its glory and fanfare nearly a century ago. Right now, this most fabulous of hotels appears to be in good hands, which means America's fairy-tale castle will continue to provide happy endings for its guests for a long time to come.

List of Awards

Some of The Plaza Hotel's many, many public honorings:

World Travel Awards: 2000 World's Leading Hotel
  1999 World's Leading Hotel
  1998 World's Leading Hotel
  1997 World's Leading Hotel
  1996 World's Leading Hotel
  1995 World's Leading Hotel

Business Traveler International: Best Hotel in North America
  European Edition — 1990, 1991, 1992, 1993, 1994,
  1995, 1996, 1997, 1998, 1999, and 2000.
  North American Edition — 1990 through 2000.

Robb Report: "Best U.S. Hotel" — 1993, 1994, 1995, 1996,
  1997

Corporate & Incentive Travel Magazine — Award of Excellence
  1990, 1991, 1992, 1993, 1994, 1995, 1996, 1997,
  1998, 1999, and 2000.

International Airline Passenger Association — IAPA: Best Hotel
  in North America '97

Gourmet Magazine — #2 Hotel in New York City

Index

OTHER NEW YORK AND TRAVEL TITLES FROM
APPLAUSE THEATRE AND CINEMA BOOKS . . .

SEATS

150 SEATING PLANS TO
NEW YORK METRO AREA THEATRES,
CONCERT HALLS & SPORTS STADIUMS
by Sandy Millman

"Great, vital information for every theatre-goer."
— Richmond Shepard, ed., *Performing Arts Insider*

A "must-have" for theatre afficionados, this book shows the location of seats in Broadway, off-Broadway, off-off Broadway theatres, and in New York metro area theatres in New York State, Connecticut, and New Jersey.

Easy to use, with color-coded price ranges, SEATS also features seating charts for major concert halls and the area's sports arenas.

Paperback • $15.95
ISBN: 1-55783-301-X • Item: 00314401

LONDON
THEATRE WALKS

THIRTEEN WALKING TOURS TO LONDON
THEATRE SITES PAST AND PRESENT

by Jim DeYoung and John Miller
Photos by Nathan Silver

• **Thirteen walks easily accessible to public
transport • Over 100 photos • Detailed maps
accompany each walk**

"If all the world's a stage, then surely London
holds the orchestra seating. Consider this book the
usher who directs you there." — *Chicago Tribune*

"The book is a nice combination of scholarly detail
and juicy gossip and is a good choice for fans of
the theatre." — *Associated Press*

Paperback • $14.95
ISBN: 1-55783-280-3 • Item: 00314255

ABOUT THE AUTHOR

WARD MOREHOUSE III is the author of *The Waldorf-Astoria: America's Gilded Dream*. He served as Broadway columnist for the New York *Post* from 1994 to 1998 and is currently a contributing reporter to the paper. He is a New York-based theatre critic and theatre feature writer for the *Christian Science Monitor* and has been a contributor to People.com, Inside.com and Reuters news service. As a playwright, his most recent production, *If It Were Easy*, which he co-wrote with Stewart Lane, was presented off-Broadway. He lives in New York with his wife and son.